Simply Beckett

Simply Beckett

KATHERINE WEISS

SIMPLY CHARLY
NEW YORK

Contents

Praise for *Simply Beckett*   vii

Other *Great Lives*   ix

Series Editor's Foreword   x

Preface   xi

Acknowledgements   xvi

Introduction: "Astride of a grave and a difficult birth": Samuel Beckett's beginning   1

1. *Le Kid, Human Wishes, Eleuthéria*: "we might well ring down the curtain."   11

2. *Waiting for Godot* and *Endgame*: Place and History on the Absurdist Stage   20

3. *Krapp's Last Tape, That Time, Ohio Impromptu*: Remembering That Time, That Place   36

4. *All That Fall, Happy Days, Footfalls, Not I*: "Spared Love": The Trauma of Being Seen; the Trauma of Being Unseen   57

5. Acts without words: Avoiding the danger zone in Beckett's *Act Without Words I, Act Without Words II, Film, Quad*, and *What Where*   79

6. Beckett's Legacy   94

Endnotes   101

Sources   107

Suggested Reading   115

About the Author   120

A Word from the Publisher   121

Praise for *Simply Beckett*

"*Simply Beckett* is simply wonderful. Katherine Weiss distills down Beckett's life and work into a knowledgeable, compelling, and compact book which is well researched while remaining thoroughly accessible. Sip from *Simply Beckett* in stages or down it in one dose. Then use it as a gateway for your return visit or for your first trip into Beckett's potent work."
    –Graley Herren, Professor of English, Xavier University

"*Simply Beckett* lucidly places all of Beckett's work for the theater in its historical and cultural contexts, with special attention to Beckett's Irish roots. The story *Simply Beckett* tells is thereby a compelling drama in itself informed by cutting-edge work on Beckett and history. This wonderful book tells the powerful story of how trauma, memory, place, and the experience of exile were woven by Beckett into uncompromising and moving works of theatrical art."
    –Robert Reginio, Professor of English, Alfred University and editor of *Samuel Beckett and Contemporary Art*

"In this engaging new study, Katherine Weiss traces Beckett's artistic sensibility and complex brand of 'simplicity' through his Irish heritage, as she explores his work in dialogue with biography and history as ironic sites of personal, historical, and political failure."
    –Annette J. Saddik, Professor of Theatre and Literature, City University of New York

"Katherine Weiss's vivid new book brings together reflections on Beckett's life with close attention to his revolutionary theatre practice. The result is a fresh take on both sets of materials that acts as a compelling introduction to an author of enduring significance."

–Laura Salisbury, Professor in Medicine & English Literature, University of Exeter

"Katherine Weiss' *Simply Beckett* is a beautifully written book, one brimming with fresh critical insights. What is obvious is her utter command of her material. As part of the Simply Charly series, the book is designed for university students and theatergoers, but, in fact, it also appeals to scholars long familiar with Beckett's work. Drawing on history, politics, trauma, and memory, Weiss leads the reader through Beckett's plays in clear, engaging prose. In sum, Weiss' book has the reach and depth to make it one of the more important coordinates in Beckett scholarship."

–Matthew Roudané, Regents' Professor of English and Theater, Georgia State University

"Three cheers for *Simply Beckett*, a welcome addition to the field of Beckett Studies, and a wonderful introduction to Beckett's theatrical work. In clear, accessible prose, Katherine Weiss takes the reader through Beckett's entire dramatic oeuvre in five brisk chapters. Weiss's lucid writing and meticulous research transforms these texts, sometimes labeled 'impenetrable', into fascinating, thought-provoking revelations on the singular genius of Beckett's theatre. *Simply Beckett* is required reading for anyone who expresses even a passing curiosity about this literary titan."

–Natka Bianchini, author of *Samuel Beckett's Theatre in America* and Professor of Theatre, Loyola University

Other *Great Lives*

Simply Austen by Joan Klingel Ray

Simply Beckett by Katherine Weiss

Simply Beethoven by Leon Plantinga

Simply Chaplin by David Sterritt

Simply Chekhov by Carol Apollonio

Simply Chomsky by Raphael Salkie

Simply Chopin by William Smialek

Simply Darwin by Michael Ruse

Simply Descartes by Kurt Smith

Simply Dickens by Paul Schlicke

Simply Edison by Paul Israel

Simply Einstein by Jimena Canales

Simply Eliot by Joseph Maddrey

Simply Euler by Robert E. Bradley

Simply Faulkner by Philip Weinstein

Simply Fitzgerald by Kim Moreland

Simply Freud by Stephen Frosh

Simply Gödel by Richard Tieszen

Simply Hegel by Robert L. Wicks

Simply Hitchcock by David Sterritt

Simply Joyce by Margot Norris

Simply Machiavelli by Robert Fredona

Simply Napoleon by J. David Markham & Matthew Zarzeczny

Simply Nietzsche by Peter Kail

Simply Nietzsche by Jack Jordan

Simply Tolstoy by Donna Tussing Orwin

Simply Stravinsky by Pieter van den Toorn

Simply Turing by Michael Olinick

Simply Wagner by Thomas S. Grey

Simply Wittgenstein by James C. Klagge

Series Editor's Foreword

S imply Charly's "Great Lives" series offers brief but authoritative introductions to the world's most influential people–scientists, artists, writers, economists, and other historical figures whose contributions have had a meaningful and enduring impact on our society.

Each book provides an illuminating look at the works, ideas, personal lives, and the legacies these individuals left behind, also shedding light on the thought processes, specific events, and experiences that led these remarkable people to their groundbreaking discoveries or other achievements. Additionally, every volume explores various challenges they had to face and overcome to make history in their respective fields, as well as the little-known character traits, quirks, strengths, and frailties, myths and controversies that sometimes surrounded these personalities.

Our authors are prominent scholars and other top experts who have dedicated their careers to exploring each facet of their subjects' work and personal lives.

Unlike many other works that are merely descriptions of the major milestones in a person's life, the "Great Lives" series goes above and beyond the standard format and content. It brings substance, depth, and clarity to the sometimes-complex lives and works of history's most powerful and influential people.

We hope that by exploring this series, readers will not only gain new knowledge and understanding of what drove these geniuses, but also find inspiration for their own lives. Isn't this what a great book is supposed to do?

Charles Carlini, Simply Charly
New York City

Preface

When asked recently by a Medievalist scholar what my research was on, I said, "Samuel Beckett." She paused before responding with "now, *he* was a terrifying genius!" A genius, indeed, with a stern face whose wrinkles spoke of the intensity of his thoughts and work, even though he rarely spoke of his work. A brilliant Irish novelist, playwright, short story writer, theater director, and poet who wrote in nearly all creative media and who was a professional, directing his plays for stage and television. *Simply Beckett*, however, aims to dispel the "terrifying" image associated with this literary genius—the view that Beckett is too difficult, too theoretical, and too philosophical for the non-academic reader and viewing audience.

As is evidenced in his letters to actors and directors, Beckett (April 13, 1906–December 22, 1989) wished for his work to speak to audiences emotionally rather than intellectually. He hoped his plays, particularly, struck a nerve, making us cringe as well as laugh, disturbing our content lives. Despite this, audiences and readers cannot separate their emotional responses from questions about what they have witnessed. We want to know the who, where, what, and why. We want to make sense of what we see and what we feel. *Simply Beckett* offers a way into Beckett's plays, beginning with biographical and historical material to make theoretical questions about history, memory, and trauma accessible to all readers.

Beckett's complete body of work is too vast to address in a slim volume such as *Simply Beckett*. What I offer instead is a focus on Beckett's plays, grouping them in terms of themes that Beckett kept returning to throughout his career. It is also through his first staged play, *Waiting for Godot*, that most of us come to know Beckett. Even those who have never seen the play have certainly come across the memes depicting two shabbily dressed men waiting by a tree—an image that comes straight from the play itself. *Simply Beckett* hopes to help its readers discover Beckett the playwright through his plays. The introduction to *Simply Beckett*, "Astride of a grave and a difficult birth": Samuel Beckett's beginning," provides a brief look into the early years that shaped his adulthood and key moments of his life. Its purpose is not to delve into the plays, but rather to outline Beckett's life. Despite the luxury and privilege in which Beckett grew up, he felt misunderstood and like an outcast from the start. His awareness that birth begins the crawl towards death is not just applicable to the human body. The Ireland of his youth—a dying nation which experienced a rebirth in the 1920s—was a place that became impotent and ignorant in its conservatism. While avoiding political commentary in his works, Beckett was very much aware of the new political starts in the first half of the 20th century—new beginnings that led to fresh graves. For Beckett, World War II was a turning point, a catastrophe that haunted his works. Essentially, Beckett's disgust with birth and conception, which humorously made its way into his prose, shades each work throughout Beckett's seven-decade writing career.

Chapter 1: *Le Kid, Human Wishes, Eleuthéria*: "...we might well ring down the curtain," explores Beckett's three abandoned adventures with the theater, aborted attempts prior to his major play, *Waiting for Godot*. During Beckett's brief teaching career at Trinity College Dublin, he went to the Abbey Theatre to see plays by his fellow Irish authors. The works of J.M. Synge and Sean O'Casey particularly caught his eye. Perhaps the hours he spent at the theater sparked his interest in playwriting. However, Beckett soon lost interest in *Le Kid* (1931), which he and fellow lecturers at Trinity College Dublin adapted from Pierre Corneille's 17th-century play titled *Le Cid*. Corneille's tragedy turned into a burlesque and was renamed after Charlie Chaplin's silent film, *The Kid*. Five years later, Beckett found himself at a standstill with a one-act *Human Wishes*; and although he completed *Eleuthéria* (1947), he decided against having it staged or published during his lifetime. What these early and aborted starts gave Beckett, however, was the momentum to continue and the ability to recognize what worked on stage.

The chapters that follow explore place and history in various ways to paint a compelling portrait of Beckett. Early scholars needlessly obscured his work by insisting that the plays occur outside of any recognizable space or time. This line of thought is debunked in the second chapter, *Waiting for Godot* and *Endgame*: Place and History on the Absurdist Stage. The chapter takes readers through the specific references to places in both plays, showing how references to the Eiffel Tower, Lake Como, and the Ardennes, for example, suggest that these plays are not without historical markers. These mentions of real places reveal that Beckett's plays are post-World War II texts in which the once-recognizable landscapes have become wastelands. What remains are the fragmented memories of the injured and traumatized characters on stage. *Waiting for Godot* and *Endgame* start the exploration of history, memory, and trauma.

In *Krapp's Last Tape*, *That Time*, *Ohio Impromptu*: Remembering That Time, That Place, the importance of place linked with memories is continued. By including three plays that span from the late 1950s to the early 1980s, I hope readers will see that Beckett's work is not moving towards a resolution. Like his plays which defy linear structures, his body of work explores themes rather than moves to understand them. The nearly silent men in the plays discussed in Chapter 3 are all storytellers who seek to remember defining moments in their lives. Each is a failure: Krapp is a failed lover and writer, and the Listeners in the two later works are elderly, lonely, silent men. In *That Time*, the Listener is a vagrant. In *Ohio Impromptu*, the Listener is an exile. Each of these men have run out of stories to tell. In these works, Beckett aligned storytelling and writing about the past and trauma with impotence and isolation.

While Beckett's body of work is sometimes thought of as male-centered, his oeuvre contains several plays specifically about women and written for actresses, as will be explored in Chapter 4. *All That Fall*, *Happy Days*, *Footfalls*, *Not I*: "Spared Love": The Trauma of Being Seen and Being Overlooked explores four of these plays spanning nearly two decades and set in Ireland. Moreover, these works recall the Irish tradition of Cathleen ni Houlihan, the embodiment of Irish nationalism who transforms from an aged woman into a young beauty when men dedicate themselves to renewing the struggle for independence. Believing that the Republic of Ireland had become a place where intellectual thought was throttled or left to rot, Beckett created plays in which the women are old hags and frail ghosts–no longer able to bear children. He carried the traces of Cathleen ni Houlihan with him, but the female characters he created were traumatized. Each has a story that hints at sexual violation while still calling out for love.

Simply Beckett moves from biography (the time, events, and places that Beckett experienced) to questions about how historical events such as World War II and the Holocaust produced trauma that impacted memory. Chapter 5: Acts without words: Avoiding the danger zone in Beckett's *Act Without Words I, Act Without Words II, Film, Nacht und Träume, Quad,* and *What Where* goes even further, noting that trauma may exist without enough traces to identify what caused it in the first place. Beckett's mimes are examples of characters who have been set in motion by something, possibly some traumatic–though unknown–event that still haunts them. Instead, like the characters in *What Where,* the audience is left asking what happened and where.

In a sense, Beckett's plays are nostalgic. Although they are visually and structurally daring, they are essentially concerned with the past–how it shapes us and how it assaults us. Fittingly, *Simply Beckett* concludes with a review of the legacy this great writer left behind. He inspired works of scholarship, providing academic and literary critics with complex works to puzzle over. Beckett's work, too, has inspired writers, musicians, and artists, all attempting to learn from him and incorporate some of his experimentation in their own work. However, most importantly, Beckett's work speaks to readers and audiences; the student who emails me asking to know more, or the audience member contemplating with furrowed brow the emotional experience she has just had. Beckett's plays inspire the utterance of unknowing and the continued struggle to learn, even if that struggle ends in failure.

Katherine Weiss
Johnson City, Tennessee

Acknowledgements

I wish to thank Charles Carlini for including my work in the Simply ... series, a collection of books that have been widely successful and enjoyable to read.

I am grateful to East Tennessee State University, especially to my students, colleagues, and Dean Gordon Anderson, for their support and intellectual rigor both of which helped in the research and writing of this book. The funding and time allotted to me to do this research and the university's library resources have been invaluable.

With sincere gratitude to Elizabeth Weiss and Nick Pope for being willing to proofread *Simply Beckett*.

Special thanks go to Jutta Brederhoff and Joachim Leisegang for their support and mentorship, to Erika Nolan for her friendship and to Nina for putting a spell on me.

Introduction: "Astride of a grave and a difficult birth": Samuel Beckett's beginning

In the Irish village of Foxrock in 1903, William "Bill" Beckett, of the successful quantity surveying company Beckett & Metcalf, had a house built for his bride Maria "May" Roe Beckett on the corner of Brighton Road and Terrymount Avenue. The couple had been married for two years and Frank, their firstborn, was one year old when the family moved from Pembroke Road into the three-story Tudor-style home they called "Cooldrinagh," which had a veranda, croquet lawn, large garden, and tennis court. It is in this fine house that Samuel Barclay Beckett was born on April 13, 1906. His childhood in Cooldrinagh would be filled with comfort and luxury, a place where a boy could play with his brother and three cousins who would join the family in 1914. Deirdre Bair, author of *Samuel Beckett: A Biography*, recalled that Beckett had said that his childhood was "uneventful," adding that he "had little talent for happiness" (14).

Both Bill and May came from affluent families. Bill's father William and his uncle James were master builders who constructed important civic buildings, such as Ireland's National Library and National Museum. Bill was a good-natured man who had a firm hand on the business world. The Becketts descended from the French Protestant Huguenots. The Roes, according to Beckett, had come from a Quaker background. His mother was the daughter of a grain business owner. Biographers James Knowlson and Deirdre Bair disagree as to why May began working as a nurse. She was educated and brought up in social standing that would normally warrant only volunteerism, but May took up work as a nurse at the Adelaide Hospital in Dublin. Bair argues that May's "high spirits and penchant for the unusual made her a constant discipline problem" at Moravian

Mission School, causing her to "put her skills to more formal use and set off for Dublin where she shocked everyone by taking a job and getting a salary" (8). Knowlson, on the other hand, revealed in *Damned to Fame: The Life of Samuel Beckett* that the decision was driven by the death of May's father. Knowlson discovered that the family grain business "took a serious downward turn in the early 1880s" and the death of Samuel Roe left the family with his debts to pay (25). The decision to become a nurse changed May's life: she met her future husband at the hospital where she worked in 1901. Bill was recovering there from an unknown illness which is believed to have been influenza or pneumonia.

April 13, 1906, the day of Samuel Barclay Beckett's birth, was Good Friday and Friday the 13th, meshing the crucifixion of Christ with the day believed by some to bring bad luck in the western world.[1] Religion and superstition were merged into one for the author; throughout his life, he was plagued by the awareness of having been born on such an unfortunate day. This sense of dread and failure from the first breath is repeatedly present in Beckett's prose and plays. In his fiction, conception and birth are often recollected with disparaging remarks and macabre humor. In the opening of "First Love," his short story of 1946 which depicts a homeless man who believes he finds love and moves in with a young woman he first calls Lulu and then renames as Anna, the narrator expresses this displeasure with birth: "For the date of my own birth, I repeat, my own birth, I have never forgotten, I never had to note it down, it remains graven in my memory, the year at least, in figures that life will not easily erase" (25). Here, the phrase "will not easily erase" reveals that the narrator wishes he could wipe out that day. And, in the word "graven" Beckett aligned birth with death. Birth, for Beckett, marks the moment when we begin our descent into the grave. Despite the grimness of the narrator's statement, humor is present when he claims to never forget the date. But he is quick to correct himself, as he has forgotten all but the year of his birth.

Beckett again injected humor into his prose when he had the

narrator recall learning that his partner, Lulu (who he also calls Anna), is pregnant:

> She offered me a side view of her belly. She even undressed, no doubt to prove she wasn't hiding a cushion under her skirt, and then of course for the pure pleasure of undressing. Perhaps it's just wind, I said, by way of consolation. She gazed at me with her big eyes whose colour I forget, with one big eye rather, for the other seemed riveted on the remains of the hyacinth. The more naked she was the more cross-eyed. Look, she said, stooping over her breasts, the haloes are darkening already. I summoned up my remaining strength and said, Abort, abort, and they'll blush like new. (44)

The narrator's suggestion that Lulu's expanded belly is just intestinal gas and his disgust and attempts at fleeing his responsibility by encouraging her to seek an abortion so that her darkening nipples will return to their youthful blush, reveal Beckett's own anxiety over conception and birth. Beckett claimed to have remembered being trapped in his mother's womb, as told in James and Elizabeth Knowlson's *Beckett Remembering/Remembering Beckett: A Centenary Celebration*. This, along with the poverty later in life and political upheaval he witnessed as an adult, led to his decision not to father any children of his own. While the tone in his short story "First Love" is one of dark humor, in his drama there is little laughter when characters reflect on birth. For example, as early as in *Waiting for Godot*, a play about two tramps who wait endlessly for a Mr. Godot, a man they have never met, and who are visited by two other tramps, birth is aligned with an image of death. Pozzo, the bourgeois tyrant who has lost his sight, responds out of frustration with the word "when," to the tramps, Didi and Gogo: "They give birth astride of a grave, the light gleams an instant, then it's night once more" (83). Moments later, Didi ruminates to himself: "Astride of a grave and a difficult birth. Down in the hole, lingering lay, the gravedigger puts on the forceps. We have time to grow old. The air is full of our cries" (84). Still preoccupied with birth and death years later, Beckett opened his 1979 work, A Piece of Monologue, with "Birth was the death of him" (425). The character standing alone on stage in this short play continues to recollect the horror of youth: "Ghastly grinning ever since. Up at the lid to come. In cradle and crib. At suck first fiasco. With the first totters. From mammy to nanny and back. All the way. Bandied back and forth. So ghastly grinning on" (425). In this one-man show, the images of an eerily grinning child and the description of his first failure—the act of feeding at the mother's breast—are haunting images that collapse birth into death in ways that are reminiscent of W. B. Yeats's troubling images of the soul being "fastened to a dying animal" in the poem "Sailing to Byzantium." The human body for Yeats, another Irish author who won Nobel Prize for literature, is a "paltry thing," "a tattered coat upon a stick." Familiar with his countryman's poetry, and the paintings of W. B.'s brother, Jack B. Yeats, Beckett carried forth a tradition of Irish arts, a tradition consumed with images of poverty, acts of violence, and the birth of a nation. Yet, despite the similarities, none of Yeats's mysticism or nationalism makes its way into the works of Samuel Beckett.

For Beckett, being born and living was a struggle, but not one marked with spiritual turmoil as it was for Yeats, financial hardship as it was for Tennessee Williams's family,[2] or with violence as it was for the American playwright Sam Shepard. Beckett's view appears to be inherently Irish. Like James Joyce and W. B. Yeats, he was troubled by a sense of body and place, and haunted by Foxrock, the Dublin suburb he left behind. Ireland, as Seán Kennedy reveals in "Does Beckett Studies Require a Subject? Mourning Ireland in the Texts for Nothing," resurfaces as a site of trauma in Beckett's work. For Joyce, the human body and Ireland became a place to defy the conservative Catholic space and provincialism of nation and family. He celebrated sexuality in the Penelope chapter in Ulysses, for example. In Yeats, too, Ireland appears in the most uncommon spaces as, for instance, when he sought to transcend "the pavement grey" of London's Fleet Street. The persona of "The Lake Isle of

Innisfree" transports himself to the isle, as is evident in the concluding line: "I hear it in the deep heart's core."

Childhood memories

For Beckett, however, the decaying body and the Ireland of his childhood were sites of impotence and ignorance–of personal, historical, and political failure. Beckett's memories of his childhood were peppered with conflicts, with his devout and stern mother and his kind father. He often recollected walks in the Dublin Hills with his dad, which are memorialized in the pages of his late novel *Company*. In a more daunting way (as in his first completed but unproduced play *Eleuthéria*), he also remembered nightmares of being pressured to jump off the raised mass of land at Forty Foot into the Bay at Sandycove. Memories of his mother, however, were less kind. James Knowlson, Beckett's authorized biographer, wrote that "May Beckett had very strict standards of behavior and the children had to conform or risk her anger and punishment" (Damned to Fame 39). Her standards did not lessen as Beckett grew older; May's judgement over Beckett's life choices, such as living with Suzanne Déchevaux-Dumesnil for many years before marrying her, have been recorded by Knowlson. After reading some of Beckett's writing, his mother threw the 25-year-old struggling writer out of the family home. Thereafter, the theme of eviction and the distain for the bourgeois is intensified in many of Beckett's works. In his plays and prose, women are often depicted as devout and difficult women. They are overpowering and demanding, and they are tied to strict social conventions. However, Beckett did not despise his mother. In *Krapp's Last Tape*, the audience hears the voice of a younger Krapp, the character the play features, relieved when he realizes that his mother's suffering has ended as she quietly passes away.

Beckett would become one of the most famous dramatists,

bravely raising questions in his early plays about religious doctrines. A non-believer himself, he would return to culturally significant images for the Irish, such as Evensong and Vespers, as he would remember places, even when not identifying them. An Irish emigrant in France, Beckett embodied a memory of place—a deeply buried memory that nonetheless emerged from the decrepit and often paralyzed characters in his pages and on the stage.

Knowlson and Bair both agree that neither May nor Bill was an intellectual. However, the Becketts did offer Samuel and Frank an intellectually and physically stimulating childhood. Bill was his sons' favorite because of his interest in swimming, walking, and sports. Each night he read pot-boilers, but despite the lack of intellectual value in these books, the boys saw reading as an enjoyable and relaxing pastime. May, on the other hand, was passionate about animals, owning dogs and donkeys, primarily. Her sensitivity to animals must have softened the otherwise sterner parent. She demanded that the boys attend Tullow Parish with her each Sunday, while their father usually went to church only on holidays.

While May and Bill may have lacked the intellectual rigor that Beckett would later embody, Cooldrinagh was visited by cultured relatives, and Beckett and Frank were sent to the finest schools. The children's nurse, Bridget, "was a friendly, loquacious Catholic, rich in stories, folktales, and homespun wisdom," according to Knowlson (35). Beckett's aunt Cissie played the piano beautifully and her friend, Dorothy Elvery, was a talented photographer who posed the three-year-old Samuel with his mother in a photograph and later in a painting called "Bedtime" (Bair 17 and Knowlson 29).

From 1920 to 1923, Beckett followed his brother when his parents sent him to board at Portora Royal School Enniskillen; these years were troubling because of the Irish Civil War. Prior to being boarded, the Beckett brothers were schooled in Dublin—first at a private academy run by Miss Ida Elsner, and then at a preparatory school, Earlsfort House School, where they learned, among other things, French. Samuel was unhappy at Portora, as witnessed from his school cricket photographs reproduced in both Knowlson's

Damned to Fame and Eoin O'Brien's *The Beckett Country*. He felt like an outsider in the Protestant school where another Irish writer, Oscar Wilde, had been a student from 1864 until 1871. But unlike Wilde, Beckett was not a good student; his grades, even in French and Latin, were mediocre. He was much more interested in sports than in academic learning. In her biography, Bair noted that all of Beckett's accolades at Portora were tied to his athleticism.

Beckett's "suicidal behavior," as Knowlson calls it, "probably only reflected along with a child's failure to recognize his own morality, Beckett's quickly acquired passion for diving" (38). As a child, Beckett was often covered in bruises as he flung himself out of trees, and once even threw a match into an empty kerosene can. His fearless behavior must have also been a contributing factor to his excellence in sports. Unafraid of being harmed, Beckett went for the goals. As a writer, too, he seemed unafraid to experiment. In essence, each time he wrote, he dived into depths unknown without the hesitation that comes with fear.

"Quietly political"

While it is tempting to believe that his parents wished to shield Beckett from Ireland's upheavals, they chose Portora for its academics. Regardless, Beckett became "quietly" political later in life. Unlike fellow Dubliners George Bernard Shaw and Brendan Behan, whose plays bore witness to their political positions and who spoke out against political injustice, Beckett kept his work with the French Resistance and his support for other causes to himself and those close to him. What thoughts the adolescent Beckett had about Ireland's fight for independence is unknown. But knowing that Ireland had become a nation where conservative Catholicism took the place of English colonialism, where Adolf Hitler was quietly supported, and where progressive and experimental literature was banned, Beckett was determined to remain in France even during World War II.

Ireland's independence from England was only partial. Not only are six counties in the north still under England's rule, but also the Republic of Ireland that Beckett knew became a repressive, conservative place that he and many other writers fled. This brave new Ireland did not tolerate James Joyce either, and its president, Eamon de Valera, sympathized with Adolf Hitler's Germany to the extent that he wrote a eulogy for Germany's Führer. Ireland's neutrality during World War II was troubling for Beckett and other Irish writers, such as Elizabeth Bowen. In a 1956 interview with the *New York Times*, Beckett went as far as to say, "I prefer France at war to Ireland at peace."

Beckett, like his characters who continually respond to despair by simply continuing to live out their lives, looked forward to the future that would free him from Ireland. His escape from Ireland in 1931 was obvious years before he permanently relocated to France in 1937. His choice of study, Modern Languages at Trinity College Dublin, set him on a path similar to Joyce's. Focusing his studies on the language and literature of France and Italy, Beckett also learned enough Spanish to translate poetry for Octavio Paz's *Mexican Poetry*, and enough German to travel to Germany with an urgency to see artworks before the Nazis confiscated the cultural riches as Degenerate Art.[3]

During his studies, Beckett developed professional relationships with mentors such as Thomas Rudemose-Brown, who recommended him for the prestigious fellowship to teach English at Ecole Normale in Paris. To his parents' dismay, Beckett would find that teaching did not suit him. What had, however, been more to his liking was the cultural climate of Paris. He met literary figures like Gertrude Stein and his compatriot James Joyce, whose work he was already familiar with. He would write his friend, Axel Kaun, who he met during his travels through Germany, attempting to identify his own writing style by juxtaposing Stein's and Joyce's in a letter dated 1937. Paris served as a space where Beckett broadened his literary and artistic circles, allowing him to get nearer to his artistic expression of challenging the very conventions of language, dictions, grammar, and style, as he noted in his letter to Kaun.[4] Beckett would have to return to Dublin after his teaching fellowship ended, but resolved to move permanently to Paris, where his literary life would thrive. By the time the Nazis invaded France, Beckett had made Paris his permanent residence. All Beckett's plays were written after his return to France. *Eleuthéria*, his unproduced first play, was written in 1947, and *En attendant Godot*, or *Waiting for Godot* in English—the first of many of Beckett's masterfully produced plays—was written shortly thereafter. It is interesting to note that both were composed after World War II, and specifically after Beckett's return from his work with the Irish Red Cross. After the war ended, Beckett traveled to Dublin to visit his mother but in doing so, he found he could not return so easily to Paris, where Suzanne Déchevaux-Dumesnil was awaiting him. His ticket back was by joining the Irish Red Cross; Beckett was sent to the town of Saint-Lô, Normandy, to aid in the reconstruction efforts there. The experience of helping to rebuild a hospital and provide supplies for the town's residents had a profound effect on Beckett. He would remain in France, dividing his time between Paris and Ussy-sur-Marne, until his death in 1989.

1. *Le Kid, Human Wishes, Eleuthéria*: "we might well ring down the curtain."

Although Beckett did not begin writing for the stage until 1940, his interest in drama dates back to his college days at Trinity College, Dublin. He went to the theater regularly as a student and later a lecturer, and the plays he saw in part shaped his aesthetics. The set and the two tramps (father and son) of W. B. Yeats's 1939 play *Purgatory* are reminiscent of *Waiting for Godot* in which the tramps, two friends by the name of Estragon and Vladimir (or, as they refer to one another, Gogo and Didi) wait on a country road that has a stone and a nearly dead tree as its only defining features. In addition to being influenced by Yeats's dramatic writings, Beckett saw John Millington Synge's plays, most notably *Playboy of the Western World*, *The Well of the Saints*, and *The Tinker's Wedding*, when they were revived for Dublin's Abbey Theatre. Beckett's authorized biographer, James Knowlson, recalled that Beckett felt Synge's plays "had influenced his own theatre most of all." "Synge's unusual blend of humour and pathos, his stark but resilient tragicomic vision, his imaginative power, and clear-sighted pessimism. The rich texture and vitality of Synge's theatrical language and the striking, bold, simplicity of his verbal and visual imagery," were aspects of Synge's dramatic works that spoke to Beckett, Knowlson wrote. He enjoyed Christy's gallant tale of murdering his father, an act admired by the townspeople in *Playboy of the Western World;* elements of Beckett's joy in such tales turn up in Pozzo's (*Waiting for Godot*) and Hamm's (*Endgame*) attempts to capture the attention of their listeners. The Rooneys and other townspeople portrayed in Beckett's first radio play, *All That Fall*, are much like the blind couple and the humorously cruel townsfolk in Synge's *The Well of the Saints*, as well

Le Kid, Human Wishes, Eleuthéria:
"we might well ring down the

as the violent and strange folk glorifying Christy Mahon's tale of murder in *Playboy of the Western World*.

The work of the Irish dramatist Sean O'Casey, too, left its mark on Beckett. As a young man still dabbling with the idea of being a scholar, Beckett wrote a short book review of O'Casey's *Windfalls*, a collection of poetry, short stories, and one-act plays. While Beckett found fault with the aesthetics of O'Casey's poetry and short stories, he praised his short dramatic texts. In the review, Beckett noted: "Mr O'Casey is a master of knockabout in this very serious and honourable sense–that he discerns the principle of disintegration in even the most complacent solidities, and activates it to their explosion" (82). This review reveals Beckett's deep understanding of O'Casey's dramatic form. He was, indeed, a master of slapstick, as evidenced by the characters Joxer and the Captain in his play, *Juno and the Paycock*. What appears initially as vaudevillian fun in O'Casey's play, however, moves into the social fabric that is falling apart until it explodes into the dramatic finale. The horrors of poverty, the Easter Rebellion, and Irish Civil War scar the characters in O'Casey's plays.

Beckett's analysis of O'Casey as an artist of "disintegration" echoes his own aesthetic. We witness in Beckett's plays a tone that grows darker from one act to another and from one play to another. Beckett took this technique of disintegration beyond the demise in action in the plot. The character's body is disintegrated into fragments, as found in his later plays such as *Not I* and *Footfalls*, and the written word becomes increasingly minimalist in his prose and drama. Beckett went on to praise O'Casey's *Juno and the Paycock*, calling it

> his best work so far ... because it communicates most fully this dramatic dehiscence, mind and world come asunder in irreparable dissociation–'chassis' (the credit of having readapted Aguecheek and Belch in Joxer and the Captain being incidental to the larger credit of having dramatised the slump in the human solid).[1]

12 | Le Kid, Human Wishes, Eleuthéria: "we might well ring down the curtain."

Beckett's insight into the antics of the Captain and Joxer, the drunken father and his neighbourly buddy, is important. He saw these impoverished men living in a cramped Dublin tenement house during the Irish Civil War and who, despite the destitution of their families, avoid work, as being likened to Sir Andrew Aguecheek and Sir Toby Belch from Shakespeare's *Twelfth Night*. In Beckett's analysis, he aligned the contemporary controversial figure of O'Casey with that of the English Bard and, as such, he attempted to canonize his fellow Irishman as well as elevate the very Irish nature of the play. Beckett's awareness of plays beyond those staged at the Abbey during his university years, as well as his support for O'Casey and Synge, aligned him, regardless of whether he intended it to, with the Abbey's mission to "find an uncorrupted and imaginative audience trained to listen by its passion for oratory," to create plays "outside all the political questions" that divided Ireland, and to provide "the freedom to experiment which is not found in theatres of English, and without which no new movement in art or literature can succeed."[2] Beckett's critique speaks to the importance of birthplace—the sounds of the dialogue and place of the tenement house. Years later in his own stage work, particularly in *Waiting for Godot*'s the tramps Didi and Gogo, as well as *Endgame*'s two central characters Hamm and Clov, he would include bodily humor—that is, both slapstick and humor that derives from digestive sounds. The humor that arises out of Beckett's male pairing, like Joxer and the Captain, results from the bickering, the tensions, and the antics that come out of a mixture of a need for companionship and rivalry with that companionship. What is more, Beckett's plays make references to specific places in the dialogue and in his character's cadence, even when the set is similarly in an unidentified location and his characters seem to be from everywhere.

Unfinished works

After returning to Trinity College Dublin from his first sojourn in Paris in 1930 to take up a teaching post, Beckett, along with other members of the Modern Languages faculty and their students, took part in his first real theatrical venture. In the winter of 1931, they prepared a variety of plays, including an adaptation of Pierre Corneille's 17th-century four-act tragedy, *Le Cid*, renamed *Le Kid*. It is tempting to conflate his participation in the plays. Beckett's friend, Georges Pelorson, who also took part in the event, recalled that Beckett's involvement in the project was minor. He rarely showed up for rehearsals and wrote little to none of the adaptation of *Le Kid*. Pelorson, however, credited Beckett with the renaming of *Le Cid*, thus merging Corneille's tragedy with Charlie Chaplin's 1921 cinematic comedy, *The Kid*.[3] Curious that the author we associate with theatrical innovation often looked toward the silent film era for inspiration. The mimes of Chaplin and Buster Keaton spoke to his sensibilities, as seen in *Waiting for Godot* and his 1964 film, aptly titled *Film*, in which Buster Keaton flees an invisible cameraman. It was another five years before Beckett tried to write a play of his own. His academic career was short; he resigned from Trinity College Dublin in December of 1931 and left Ireland—first moving to London and then traveling throughout Germany, before settling in France.

Leaving Ireland for good, Beckett tried without avail to write two plays, *Human Wishes* (1937-40) and *Eleuthéria* (1947), neither of which were published or performed during his lifetime.

Beckett began to think about writing a play that dealt with the romance and relationship between Dr. Samuel Johnson and Mrs. Hester Tharle, a woman 31 years Dr. Johnson's junior. An American theater scholar Ruby Cohn suggested in her book *A Beckett Canon*, that Beckett turned to the subject of Dr. Johnson "in a gesture of escape from a Paris imperiled by advancing Nazi armies" (107). Cohn speculated that the play remained incomplete perhaps because of

14 | Le Kid, Human Wishes, Eleuthéria: "we might well ring down the curtain."

the increasing perils Beckett and others in Paris faced in 1940. He and his partner Suzanne would soon be on the run, fleeing the Gestapo for their involvement in the Resistance. Others, such as Knowlson, have posited that Beckett abandoned *Human Wishes* because of the difficulties in carrying forward the thematic and stylistic challenges of the play (250). Beckett struggled to find a way to bring together two very different themes that emerged in the preparation for the script. How would he manage to integrate the love affair between Johnson and Mrs. Thrale and "the image of Johnson in decline, physically ill and morbidly preoccupied with his own physical deterioration, dying, and death"?[4] And how would Beckett weave in Johnson's love of the English language? To write a play about age and love is one thing; to write one set in the 18th century, which features the father of A *Dictionary of the English Language* is yet another matter entirely. In the end, Beckett abandoned *Human Wishes* after having completed a mere fragment of the script–a fragment that, ironically, does not feature Mrs. Tharle or Dr. Johnson at all. Instead, it includes other characters, such as Mrs. Williams, Mrs. Desmoulins, Miss Carmichael, Dr. Levett, and Francis Barber.

The fragment, however, gives insight into the dramatist that Beckett would become. *Human Wishes* contains Beckett's signature silences, repetitions, and bodily humor. After the first declaration, "He is late," spoken by Mrs. Desmoulins, Beckett directs "*Silence*" (155)–a stage direction that appears five times in the opening dialogue. What is more, the scene with the three women who anticipate the arrival of a late-comer is reminiscent of the three women who sit on a park bench, remembering the past and sharing gossip in Beckett's 1965 play, *Come and Go*. Beckett, who would turn his attention away from *Human Wishes* to focus on male characters on stage for the next 26 years, began with an image of three women, "*meditating*," "*knitting*," and "*reading*" (155)–a nod towards the classical Fates or the witches in *Macbeth*. While he never finished writing the scenes between Dr. Johnson and Mrs. Tharle, it is interesting to note that the problem such scenes posed became the staple of plays like *Krapp's Last Tape*, written in 1958. Once Beckett resolved to make his character an aged failed writer, he was able to continue and create *Krapp's Last Tape*. Midway through *Human Wishes*, the character named Mrs. Williams says, while she and the other women watch the drunk Mr. Levett ascend the stairs, "Words fail us" (160). In this early play, we see Beckett's struggle to express himself.[5] Beckett found that language—words—are inadequate for the characters and the playwright. He abandoned the play, only to start another in 1947.

Eleuthéria

Beckett's second attempt at writing for the stage was more successful. *Eleuthéria* was written in French and finished in less than two months. After its completion in 1947, Beckett determined to keep this play from being made public. He neither wanted the play staged nor published. Knowlson speculated that this decision was based on the "autobiographical tensions and reminiscences [which] seemed insufficiently distanced or inadequately integrated into the play" (328). Despite its autobiographical nature, *Eleuthéria*, as a Beckett expert David Pattie pointed out, reveals "Beckett's rather self-conscious attempt to draw attention to the theatricality of the play" (73). *Eleuthéria* is an interesting failure; it is about a young man by the name of Victor Krap who attempts to escape his bourgeois family and struggles to write, both without success. However, like Krap, Beckett seems to have struggled to get to the core of what he wanted to express. It takes much too long for the audience to meet Victor, and unnecessary characters enter into action. Beckett even included "An audience member" (1) in his cast of characters, reminiscent of the pre-recorded applause in *Catastrophe*, a play written in French over three decades later. However, unlike *Catastrophe*, a play in which an old, shivering man resembling a Holocaust victim is put on display by a sadistic

16 | Le Kid, Human Wishes, Eleuthéria: "we might well ring down the curtain."

director, this "audience member" is disruptive, coming onto the stage and demanding that something useful is said and the play comes to an end. With the intrusion of the audience member, Beckett drew on Luigi Pirandello's 1921 *Six Characters in Search of an Author*. Here, an audience member searches for meaning. Knowlson explained that *Eleuthéria* "reveals Beckett's attitudes toward the theatre of the past, as well as point[s] forward to his own later, highly innovative drama. The play parodies many features of traditional plays and experiments, not always happily, with more innovative techniques" (329). Despite Knowlson's and Pattie's praise, the play is too excessive for the minimalist aesthetics that would define Beckett's writing, which he was still working through. With a cast of 17 characters and a confusing plot, Beckett came to realize that the play would not find a stage because theater spaces and budgets were limited in post-World War II Europe.

The back cover of the English translation posthumously published (in 1995) boldly states that the French actor and director Roger Blin is to blame for the delay in the play's production. Legend has it that Blin favored *Waiting for Godot* over *Eleuthéria*, which would have taught Beckett that, in the post-World War II era, plays with fewer production demands would be more lucrative. Despite the play's ambitious scope, it is hard to deny that *Waiting for Godot* is the more mature work. What we find in *Eleuthéria*, however, are the traces of many of Beckett's plays to come. His stage silences are taken further than in *Human Wishes*, as are other directed cues, including Victor Krap's "Gestures of helplessness, of indifference, shrugs" (153), which recall Keaton's gestures in *Film*, and the wrapped-up pacing character in *Not I* who, upon listening to Mouth's unrelenting monologue, gestures with helpless compassion.

What we also find in *Eleuthéria* are the puns on the names which speak to Beckett's disgust with the bourgeois. M. Krap, Victor's father and a failed writer turned respectable family man with a home and butler, and his wife Mme. Krap, are distressed over their son's absence. Victor Krap, not appearing until Act Two, is in a state of withdrawal and perhaps depression, as he no longer finds meaning in life. While the plot of this family becomes farcically melodramatic, there is no denying that Beckett's Kraps are early conceptions of the failed writer in his play *Krapp's Last Tape*. Like Victor, we learn that Krapp has forsaken love and family. But M. Krapp is no better than his son or Beckett's later embodiment of this failed writer. The name itself resonates too, as Beckett seemed to be siding with the son in his disgust that all is meaningless, all is shit. Victor has "lost his taste for life" (105). In *Eleuthéria*, we get a clear picture of what the bourgeois represented for Beckett at this time. Through the names of other characters we discover that the bourgeois is made up of muck (Madame Meck) and puke (Dr. André Piouk).

Eleuthéria often speaks to the disgust with conception and birth. For the most part, the play does so in usual Beckettian terms. However, in Dr. Piouk, who self-identifies as a "psychopath" (175), we witness a more sinister manifestation of the rejection of conception and birth:

> I would prohibit reproduction. I would perfect the condom and other appliances and generalize their use. I would create a state-run corps of abortionists. I would impose the death sentence on every woman guilty of having given birth. I would drown the newborn. I would campaign in favor of homosexuality and myself set the example. And to get things going, I would encourage by every means the recourse of euthanasia without, however, making it an obligation. (43)

Dr. Piouk's extreme position is farcical—a nod to his fellow Irishman, Jonathan Swift's "A Modest Proposal," in which Swift recommended that the children of the poor be reared and sold for food consumption—eradicating hunger and poverty in one blow. However, Dr. Piouk's solution is also reminiscent of Hitler's final solution. But instead of eradicating the Jewish race, he advocates eliminating the *human* race. Dr. Piouk does not only vomit his opinions throughout the play, but also much of what he says may

18 | Le Kid, Human Wishes, Eleuthéria: "we might well ring down the curtain."

make our stomachs churn. Beckett's skill with farce made much of what Dr. Piouk spews funny.

Undeniably, *Eleuthéria* gave Beckett the momentum to write the richly sparse play, *Waiting for Godot*. From 1947 onwards, he penned 19 stage plays, the last of which, *What Where*, was written in 1985, only four years before his death.

2. *Waiting for Godot* and *Endgame*: Place and History on the Absurdist Stage

While Europe was still recovering from World War II, Beckett's *Waiting for Godot* (*En attendant Godot*) premiered in Paris at the Théâtre de Babylon in 1953. This two-act play is about two down-and-outs named Estragon (also known as Gogo) and Vladimir (also known as Didi) who spend their days together waiting for a man they call Mister Godot. Why these hobos wait for the mysterious Mister Godot is not clear. The tramps speak about the earthly and heavenly rewards he may bring with him: a warm bed, some food, or salvation. The action is simple; these two tramps banter and engage in slapstick humor as they wait until the nightfall. Gogo and Didi's tedium is interrupted in each act by visitors. Pozzo, a pompous, once affluent man, enters the stage with his manservant. The servant, ironically named Lucky, carries Pozzo's bags, as Pozzo jerks the rope around Lucky's neck and cracks a whip. After the visitation in each act, Gogo and Didi are visited by a young boy who carries with him bad news: Mister Godot will not come. They must wait another day.

Beckett, who at this time was an unknown playwright and little-known novelist, would radically change what had at that time constituted theater. Although he had already published several poems, a book of short stories, and a handful of novels, his literary output nonetheless had received little attention from critics and readers. However, his luck would change. His play about these two tramps waiting endlessly for Mister Godot ultimately led the way to his global fame. Beckett's authorized biographer, James Knowlson pointed out that by the mid-1960s, Beckett had been nominated several times already for the Nobel Prize for Literature. His work had been translated into many languages and was studied in universities throughout the world; his plays were being put on in dozens of theaters in many countries; and countless academics, many of them known to him personally, were creating a positive avalanche of books and articles on his prose and his plays (484). Amidst this flurry of success, Beckett received the Nobel Prize for Literature in 1969–an honor that he would regard as a "catastrophe" (505). He knew well that the prize would bring about requests for interviews in which he would be asked questions about his private life and the meaning of his work. Despite the impact *Waiting for Godot* had on Beckett's career, it is important to remember that for the Dubliner already in his mid-40s, who had made Paris his permanent home (much like his mentor James Joyce), this success did not come all at once. Instead, *Waiting for Godot* had a turbulent start, but grew in popularity first in off-main stage circles, and then later on the West End and Broadway stages.

Indeed, the first audiences to encounter the play did not stick around for the second act, and even academic circles rejected Beckett's genius. The first article written on the play by the outstanding scholar, then only a student, Ruby Cohn was rejected. Cohn, an American studying at the Sorbonne, saw the Paris premiere of *Waiting for Godot*. Recognizing the play's significance, she composed her first of many critical works on the playwright. Her 1959 essay, however, was turned down by the journal's editor. The response she received read: "We like your criticism, but we don't feel your author merits publishing space."[1] Cohn persisted, and her attempts to get to know Beckett's work better led to a life-long friendship with the author. Cohn knew from the start that Beckett's work merited more than just a few pages in a literary journal. Dedicating her life to his work, she became a leading authority on his stage plays, culminating in her final book on the author, *The Beckett Canon*, and the donation of her correspondence to the Beckett International Foundation housed at the University of Reading in the U.K.

In America, too, the play received a rocky start. The American director, Alan Schneider, wrote to the playwright apologetically about his failure to captivate the audience when staging the play at Miami, Florida's Coconut Grove Playhouse in 1956. Beckett responded with:

> Success and failure on the public level never mattered much to me, in fact I feel much more at home with the latter, having breathed deep of its vivifying air all my writing life up to the last couple of years. And I cannot help feeling that the success of *Godot* has been very largely the result of a misunderstanding, of various misunderstandings, and that perhaps you have succeeded better than any one else in stating its true nature. (8)

His letter to Schneider was clearly an act of kindness; but in fact, it was more than that. Beckett recognized Schneider's worth as a director who blamed not the script for the play's failure, but the production. It is obvious from the chapter "The Laugh Sensation of Two Continents" by Natka Bianchini, a professor of theater at Loyola University, that the production's failure was largely due to the producer Michael Myerberg's distrust of the simplicity of the text and his unwillingness to execute the valuable insights that Schneider brought back from his discussions with Beckett. Schneider traveled to Paris on multiple occasions to speak with Beckett, continuing his discussions with the playwright in their correspondence to ensure that he understood the author's intent. From this moment on, Beckett and Schneider formed a rich friendship, the written remains of which have been collected in Maurice Harmon's *No Author Better Serve: The Correspondence of Samuel Beckett and Alan Schneider*, and, more recently, in Natka Bianchini's *Samuel Beckett's Theatre in America: The Legacy of Alan Schneider as Beckett's American Director*.[2] Their friendship was one that explicitly involved work. As a sign of his gratitude, Beckett gave Schneider the rights to direct all his American premieres (as well as *Film*, his 1964 exploration into cinema). This is an extraordinary gesture, considering that the American debut of *Waiting for Godot* was poorly received and, as Bianchini noted, poorly staged.

"A play in which nothing happens"

In 1958, only two years after Beckett's gracious letter to Schneider, *Krapp's Last Tape*, Beckett's one-act play about a writer who could not sell copies of his book and stopped writing, was staged. Beckett's thoughts during this time were also attuned to failure and, like Schneider who took on the blame, Beckett may have believed he was doomed to fail–a playwright condemned to short-runs and empty theaters.

In his book review of *Waiting for Godot*, Irish literary critic Vivian Mercier best described the play's disappointment and, for audiences to come, its attraction, by astutely observing that Beckett had composed a play that broke from tradition:

> Its author has achieved a theoretical impossibility–a play in which nothing happens, that yet keeps audiences glued to their seats. What's more, since the second act is a subtly different *reprise* of the first, he has written a play in which nothing happens, *twice*. (29)

Mercier's review, while a clever observation that often brings a smile to today's students and scholars of drama, has been rattled off too quickly–a performance of the critic to show how well-read he/she is in Beckett studies. But if we give pause to Mercier's review, we discover that he was commenting on dramatic structure and theater conventions that today, because of Beckett, are no longer followed as strictly as they once were. In this pause, we are left wondering what was it that brought the Irish writer to pen, in his mid-life, a play which dismantles dramatic structure–a structure that hinges on something happening.

To tackle this question, we need to consider the play in dialogue with biography and history. *Waiting for Godot* was completed five years before a theater would accept the script. Suzanne Déchevaux-Dumesnil peddled the play from one theater to the next until the director and actor Roger Blin enthusiastically took it on. Thus, to associate the play only with its date of performance, 1953, would be a mistake. Beckett finished writing the work between 1947 and 1948, only a few years after World War II ended, and his stint with the Irish Red Cross in Normandy.

During World War II and the immediate post-war period, Beckett was engrossed in writing novels, namely *Watt* and, his three other novels, *Molloy*, *Malone Dies*, and *The Unnamable*, which are often referred to as *The Trilogy*. He claimed that he turned to theater as "a relief and for the sake of a challenge" after struggling with the prose fiction that had consumed most of his life in the 1930s and 1940s, according to Knowlson (328). Whether this was the true reason to start playwriting, one cannot know. What we do know is that this shift to writing plays offered its own challenges. After all, *Waiting for Godot* was not Beckett's first attempt at writing for the stage. Hence, his reason does not explain why, after abandoning theater years earlier, Beckett returned to the genre and wrote a play that challenged theater with its sheer minimalist plot, dialogue, characters, and set. In his earlier dip into playwriting, Beckett loosely based *Human Wishes* on the life of Samuel Johnson, abandoning this project in 1940. Seven years later, he returned to playwriting with *Eleuthéria*, which, as stated before, is an exhausting script with its 17 characters and lots of antics. After Suzanne unsuccessfully attempted to find a stage for *Eleuthéria*, Beckett must have begun to realize that the play was too excessive for theaters that were struggling to survive after the war.

Still saturated by a Joycean style, *Eleuthéria* is an inferior play. However, it gave Beckett the momentum to write *Waiting for Godot*—a play that begins to step away from the aesthetic influence of his mentor and friend, James Joyce. Indeed, as early as 1937, we see Beckett striving towards minimalism, rather than Joyce's "apotheosis of the word" (519), as is evident in his letter to Axel Kaun, a Berliner who the author befriended during his travels throughout Germany between 1936 and 1937. But Beckett did not cast off his debt to Joyce immediately, as is evident in the monologue which the slave by the name of Lucky gives in *Waiting for Godot*. With and after *Waiting for Godot*, Beckett increasingly moved towards the decaying minimalism he longed for. In 1956, he discussed his move away from the Joycean aesthetic with the *New York Times* contributor, Israel Shenker:

> Joyce was a superb manipulator of material–perhaps the greatest. He was making words do the absolute maximum of work. There isn't a syllable that's superfluous. The kind of work I do is one in which I'm not master of my material. The more Joyce knew the more he could. He's tending toward omniscience and omnipotence as an artist. I'm working with impotence, ignorance. I don't think impotence has been exploited in the past. There seems to be a kind of esthetic axiom that expression is an achievement–must be an achievement. My little exploration is that whole zone of being that has always been set aside by artists as something unusable–as something by definition incompatible with art.

In this statement, Beckett, perhaps unknowingly, made the distinction between the pre- and post-World War II writing, or, as some critics see it, the difference between modernism and post-modernism. It is impossible to determine whether this shift occurred because of his closeness to Joyce prior to the war, or because of the war experience itself. In fact, both may well be culprits in this change in Beckett's writing. What was this shift, exactly? Beckett's plays and prose are not simply about characters that cannot act, know, express, or produce. Instead, he redefined the creative (potent) process as one that leads nowhere and, at least on the surface, produces no thing or effect. He ultimately explored the possibilities of writing that is not "an achievement" and must not "be an achievement." Beckett's writing is that which "dares to fail" as an expressive act, as he stated art should do in "Three Dialogues"

(145); it is an act that fails at saying while expressing that which is unsayable.

Waiting for Godot and his subsequent play, *Endgame*, have too often been labeled as Absurdist or Existentialist works without a clear understanding of the works themselves. By taking a step away from these literary terms–meant to clarify but often only obscure the literary texts and stage plays–and by grounding the works back in history and biography, we discover that these plays, which resonate so deeply for incarcerated men and women, are less baffling than we imagine them to be, even in their impotence and ignorance. Incarcerated individuals understand what it is to wait, as Gogo and Didi do. *Endgame*, too, is a play that depicts characters trapped with nothing to do. The character named Clov serves a family there. He waits on Hamm, who is a boisterous disabled man confined to a wheelchair, and Hamm's parents, an elderly and disabled couple. Hamm's father Nagg and his mother Nell, having lost their legs from the knees downward, reside in separate trashcans. All four characters live in a small room with an adjacent pantry. Unlike *Waiting for Godot*, however, there is no person they hope will arrive. Instead, the tension is in Clov's threat to leave. He goes so far as to change his clothes and move towards the door, but his departure is never complete.

I would venture to guess that audiences are puzzled by these works because they are structurally so different from plays that had been staged prior to Beckett–works such as the Naturalist and Realist plays of the 19th and 20th centuries. In Beckett's rejection of this tradition, he created an aura of mystery around his work. The works of Henrik Ibsen, Anton Chekhov, and, in the 20th century, George Bernard Shaw and Terrance Rattigan have great theatrical presence. They all express political, moral, and personal dilemmas. For Beckett and some of his contemporaries, however, this theater tradition was too structured, ultimately too clean, to make sense after having been through the bombings of Europe and the horrors of the Holocaust; writers like Beckett had no words for these experiences.

"Humanity in ruins"

From James Knowlson's biography and the work of other scholars, such as Seán Kennedy, Mark Nixon, and Rob Reginio, we know about Beckett's World War II activities. While he and others living in Paris in the 1940s had escaped the devastating bombing that Germany subjected much of Europe to, the author, who had strong connections to Jewish writers and whose beloved uncle Boss Sinclair was Jewish, was deeply disturbed by France's surrender to Germany in 1940. Despite this, Beckett was unwilling to return to Ireland, whose President Eamon de Valera was a Nazi sympathizer.[3] When France surrendered to Germany, Beckett joined the French Resistance group, Gloria SMH. Shortly thereafter, this cell was betrayed. In 1942, Beckett and Suzanne fled on foot, walking for weeks and covering roughly 435 miles until they settled in Roussillon, a French farming community, a journey that is recorded in the essay "'In Love with Hiding': Samuel Beckett's War." While hiding out the rest of the war in Roussillon—which, upsettingly, was in the vicinity of a concentration camp—Beckett and Dechevaux-Demesnil worked on a farm in exchange for food. In his spare time, Beckett wrote his novel *Watt*, a maddening work that expresses the frustration he must have experienced during his years in hiding. After the war, Beckett returned to Dublin briefly to check on his elderly mother, whose health was deteriorating. The post-war climate made it difficult for Beckett to return to France. Seeing no way back to Paris, where Suzanne was awaiting him, he joined the Irish Red Cross and was sent to Saint-Lô, Normandy, a town nearly wiped out in the bombing. It is there that Beckett was faced with what he called in an unaired radio broadcast he composed, "humanity in ruins" (278).

In *Waiting for Godot* and *Endgame*, we find traces of Beckett's own waiting, his fear, and his scars from the war. As he witnessed the perseverance of humankind, he also gained a new understanding of life, the need to go on living even when our daily routines seem insignificant. In this sense, Beckett's plays explore resilience in the face of despair. These works, ultimately, reflect Beckett's experiences during World War II. However, he was always careful not to create biographical works as S. E. Gontarski in *The Intent of Undoing in Samuel Beckett's Dramatic Texts* and H. Porter Abbott in *Beckett Writing Beckett: The Author in the Autograph* have demonstrated in their careful analyses of Beckett's writing and revision process.

In *Waiting for Godot* and *Endgame*, Beckett created characters in destitute surroundings. Didi and Gogo in *Waiting for Godot* are outside, on a lonesome road with only a nearly-dead tree and a stone in their vicinity. In most productions, the tramps are road-weary, unbathed, wearing dirty and torn clothing, ill-fitting boots, and subsisting on turnips, radishes, and carrots. What is disputed, however, is whether the stage spaces in *Waiting for Godot* and *Endgame* are deracinated landscapes, places without any recognizable origin or roots, as Richard Gilman had argued in his 1974 essay for the *Parisian Review*, or whether they are rooted in history and place, as the contributors to *Samuel Beckett: Memory, History, Archive* claimed. In his insightful chapter for the collection, Rob Reginio examined the sparse 1984 German production directed by George Tabori, revealing the historical relevance of the staging which depicts the play in the rehearsal process. In the same collection, Jackie Blackman insightfully explored the traces of the Auschwitz concentration camp found throughout *Endgame*.

Diverse productions

The urge of early critics and theater professionals to think of the spaces in Beckett's works as having no historical or geographical origin speak to an avoidance of the terrible events of World War II. Perhaps Walter Benjamin's "The Storyteller," an essay that attempts to explain the avoidance of writing about World War I in fiction, holds true for Beckett in that the unspeakable atrocities of World War II seep into his plays, but do so in a way that eluded scholars. The earliest drafts of *Waiting for Godot*, according to Knowlson, name one of the tramps Lévy—a distinctly Jewish name (344), thereby locating, at least at this early stage, the play in the historical moment of World War II. Many productions since the publication of Knowlson's *Damned to Fame* have made the space less ambiguous. For example, in the 1996 Gate Theatre production directed by Michael Lindsay-Hogg and starring Barry McGovern and Frank Murphy (and which was later recorded for the *Beckett on Film* Project available on DVD), and in the 2009 London's West End production directed by Sean Matthias and starring Patrick Stewart and Ian McKellen, the sets have the appearance of being ravished by catastrophic violence, perhaps even war. In the Gate Theatre production, the stone that Gogo (played by Murphy) sits on looks less like a naturally formed stone than a mortar stone from a building—perhaps from a building that had been bombed. In the West End production, the set is clearly a theater that was bombed and abandoned. The roof and walls are gone and thus the stage has merged into the road. And, although not devastated by war, the very location of Paul Chan's 2006 production—outdoors in New Orleans's 9th Ward a year after Hurricane Katrina devastated the area—interprets the play's road in a landscape devastated by a disaster.[4] These productions were staged after Knowlson's biography was published, and thus were undoubtedly influenced by the new information Knowlson brought to light. Nevertheless, defining the space without pointing to a specific catastrophe makes for powerful performance—which still defies a theater that achieves an expressive end, as Naturalist plays of the 19th century did.

Indeed, previous productions, too, contained traits of the war. Knowlson noted that from the earliest productions, theater critics saw connections between Pozzo's treatment of Lucky and the "capo in a concentration camp brutalizing his victim with his whip" (344). Additionally, directors like George Tabori spoke about the Holocaust in terms of Germany's controversial response in the 1980s to the horrors of the war crimes—a political and intellectual quarrel known as Historikerstreit, which revolved around explaining Nazi Germany and the Holocaust in the context of German history. Reginio showed that Tabori's 1984 production situates "the questions of collective memory pressed upon histories and the German nation as a whole" and, as such, the production testified to a "coming to grips with the Holocaust" in its metatheatrical staging of the play (121; 125).

The set for *Endgame*, likewise, does not exist outside of history. As in *Waiting for Godot*, it is a destitute space. In spite of Beckett's own distaste for making the locations of his plays too specific, as the famous 1984 JoAnne Akalaitis production of *Endgame* did when she set the play in an abandoned subway car, *New York Times* reviewer Mel Gussow pointed out (in defense of Akalaitis's production) that the play can be seen as metaphorically being set in "a bunker in a world after the nuclear holocaust—a view that is supported in the text." Gussow did not elaborate on what in the text supports this assertion, but instead he argued that the director had "made a defensible scenic interpretation. One man's cell could be another's graveyard." Regardless of her intentions, Akalaitis had gone too far for Beckett to accept. In changing the location of the play, she missed what many scholars and critics have also overlooked when, perhaps too hastily, they pointed to the threat of nuclear war as a point of distress in the play. Beckett set his strange play for four actors in a barren room with very high windows, resembling both a bunker and a cellar or basement, like those that most European citizens would have sought shelter in during air raids that devastated much of Europe, including London. What exactly is happening outside the room in which Clov, Hamm, Nagg, and Nell reside in is unknown and unknowable. What is clear, however, is that the space they live in is safe, as long as there is food for them to exist on—although food, too, seems to be running low.

The characters in both plays have fond memories of the past—a past that is not associated with their current location or situation. These characters, in a sense, are displaced as Beckett and Dechevaux-Dumensnil were when they went into hiding after Gloria

SMH was exposed. Didi and Gogo have come to a place on the road where they wait each day. Despite their current place and time, they recall holding hands and looking down on Paris from the Eiffel Tower. A universally recognized historical structure, the Eiffel Tower was built in 1889 for the World's Fair. Its architect meant for the Tower to celebrate the centennial of the French Revolution. It might be a stretch to claim that this memory situates Didi and Gogo as representing goodwill ambassadors for democracy, but when juxtaposed to Pozzo and Lucky—the master and slave pair—we see a distinct contrast between Didi and Gogo's friendship (as witnessed in their embrace both in Act I and Act II) from that of the inequality and cruelty that Pozzo acts out on Lucky. What is more, while staying with Pozzo, Lucky never talks about happier days. Pozzo reminisces about Lucky's dancing[5] and his thinking (which Lucky does aloud, as though he were reciting what is on his mind) as being once beautiful, but Lucky is silent on this topic, very much like Clov in *Endgame*.

Endgame

Beckett's second staged play, *Endgame*, has many similarities with *Waiting for Godot*. Most notably, the dynamic between Hamm and Clov echoes that of Pozzo (who, too, is a ham-actor) and Lucky (who also serves and slaves for another). Moreover, in the second act of *Waiting for Godot*, Pozzo has gone blind like Hamm. But unlike *Waiting for Godot*, *Endgame* situates its master/slave relationship at the forefront and its loving pair (Nagg and Nell, who echo Gogo and Didi) in the background. Like the tramps who recall holding hands on top of the Eiffel Tower and harvesting grapes in the Rhône Valley, Nagg and Nell share memories of love on Lake Como. For them, the romantic Italian getaway was a place of fun and laughter—it is where they became engaged to be married and where Nagg shared his joke of the botched tailoring for the first time. Despite the love and laughter, the place also hinted at the danger of drowning. Nagg recalls that Nell was "in such fits that we capsized. By rights we should have been drowned":

NELL	It was because I felt happy.
NAGG	[*Indignant.*] It was not, it was not, it was my story and nothing else. Happy! Don't you laugh at it still? Every time I tell it. Happy!
NELL	It was deep, deep. And you could see down to the bottom. So white. So clean. (102)

Nagg and Nell's memory of laughter, whether out of happiness, is filled with possible disaster. Likewise, Gogo and Didi's memory of picking grapes is mired with death by drowning (as a reminder, Estragon and Vladimir are real names of Didi and Gogo):

ESTRAGON	Do you remember the day I threw myself into the Rhône?
VLADIMIR	We were grape-harvesting.
ESTRAGON	You fished me out.
ESTRAGON	That's all dead and buried. (51)

In both plays, happy memories of the past are memories of love, friendship, laughter, and, most importantly, of a possible end. Gogo and Nell dream of drowning in deep, clean, and white water rather than drowning in memories of the past, as they do in their old age. Ultimately, despite longing for an end, in both plays (and for that matter, all of Beckett's plays) there is none.

Nagg's strange denial that Nell felt happy must be understood in terms of their current context. Even Nell, who scolds Nagg for laughing at their son Hamm, says:

Nothing is funnier than unhappiness, I grant you that. But –
...

Yes, yes, it's the most comical thing in the world. And, we laugh, we laugh, with a will, in the beginning. But it's always the same thing. Yes, it's like the funny story we have heard too often, we still find it funny, but we don't laugh any more. (101)

Laughter, Nell reveals, is a complex reaction. It need not be a sign of happiness, although for Nell it was on Lake Como. However, here she reveals that unhappiness is funnier than the joke. Although she admits that unhappiness is "funny," she cautions against laughing at it. She and Nagg laugh "less heartily" (100) at their unhappy memory of losing the lower part of their legs while riding together on a tandem bicycle in the Ardennes. Interestingly, while Beckett rejected identifiable locations for the stage space in which the characters reside, they have a memory of other places that hold significant historical markers that are identifiable for the audience. The Ardennes forest and mountains are not only dangerous for the bicycling tourists Nagg and Nell, but also served the Nazis as their primary route into France.[6]

Memories and nostalgia

Although often seen as a playwright of extreme minimalism and the absurd, Beckett's plays are wrapped up in memory. He was perhaps the most nostalgic of 20th-century playwrights, even when his stage images attempted to defamiliarize the nostalgia. Often in Beckett's stage directions, the location of the road or the room remains unknown. That said, specific locations are rife in the memories of his characters. Didi and Gogo remember their time together in Paris and the Rhône Valley. Nagg and Nell remember their time on Lake Como and the Ardennes. This naming of places when nostalgically looking back, in contrast to the refusal to name the set, speaks to catastrophic destruction such as the bombing of Saint-Lô, which rendered the town unrecognizable. However, memory of better days acts as a means to defy the ruins that Beckett was confronted with. His characters embody "humanity in ruins" as they hold on to the past to help them through the present.

Although not nostalgic, Lucky is a strange figure who cannot escape the past. His "think" is a collage of personal and collective memories—memories that Beckett, Lucky, and Pozzo share—as well as historical references that an Irish or European audience would recognize. And his dance, which Gogo calls the "Scapegoat's agony" (39), but which Pozzo explains is actually Lucky imagining that he is caught in a net, recalls the atrocities of Nazi Germany. The term scapegoat is one that is forever tied to memories of the Holocaust. The image of a net, too, has historic significance; it reflects the entrapment of the death camps. And, yet, these images speak to the manner in which Beckett became inspired by the people of Saint-Lô. Rather than give in to the ruins around them, they picked up the pieces to clear the roads, and rebuild the hospital and road. Like Lucky who cannot be driven away—according to Pozzo—the inhabitants of Saint-Lô were not driven away despite the bombing and destruction of their town. Lucky, as well as Beckett's other characters, persevere despite the rubble before them, and their weary and ruined bodies.

But to call these plays hopeful or a celebration of perseverance would be going too far. Not only does the boy in *Waiting for Godot* bring news that Mister Godot "won't come" (48; 85), but also we never truly discover who the mysterious Godot is. Similarly, Clov never leaves the stage and, what is more, the boy who Clov sees from the window never arrives. Boys appear throughout Beckett's plays for stage and television, always representing absence and an image of impotence in the body of youth—a body with possibility.

The endless wait, the single most daring aspect of *Waiting for Godot*, set Beckett apart from theater traditions of his contemporaries. He was beleaguered by critics and reporters who wanted to know who Godot was. As is well known, Beckett refused to answer, claiming he did not know. It is intriguing that today's audiences accept the mystery of Godot and respond more openly to the play as they do to *Endgame*–another play in which nothing much happens. This acceptance speaks to the status of *Waiting for Godot* and *Endgame* as having found a stable position in the canon of popular and conventional theater. Both plays have been embraced by actors such as Robin Williams, Patrick Stewart, Michael Gambon, and Daniel Radcliffe, to name a few. Both plays, too, have been staged in the West End and Broadway theaters. Fortunately, however, their canonization has not diminished their expression of impotence and ignorance.

3. Krapp's Last Tape, That Time, Ohio Impromptu: Remembering That Time, That Place

After having experimented with writing for radio at the request of the BBC, Beckett created Krapp's Last Tape in 1958–a beautifully nostalgic play that is sparser than Waiting for Godot and Endgame although, in terms of its aesthetic, is more conventional than the earlier works, complicating the picture of Beckett's theatrical aesthetic and writerly progress. By reducing the number of characters on stage to the extent that often there would be only one, Beckett minimized his use of stage dialogue and action, which would continue in some of his later works. The character by the name of Krapp is nearly fixed to his desk. He is an elderly man of 69 who, each year on his birthday, records a tape in which he reflects upon the year that has gone by. On this particular birthday, the audience sees Krapp listening to a tape from his 39th birthday, the year that he ended his relationship with a young woman while out punting with her. Krapp, the audience learns, broke off the relationship to focus on becoming a writer. However, when the 69-year-old records his tape, the audience discovers that his career as a writer never amounted to much.

The characters named Reader and Listener in Ohio Impromptu (1981), a short one-act play, are two mysterious men who look as much alike as possible. This late play contains no action. The two men remain seated at a table. Reader literally reads out of a large book to Listener; the story he reads is about a lonely man who is heartbroken over his lost memories and lost love. His grief keeps him wanting to hear more of the story Reader reads. The character of Listener in *That Time* (1975) is an elderly man who seems to be lying in bed. The audience only sees his head, though. During this short one-act play, the Listener silently listens to memories of his life. As a child, he often hid from adults. As an adult, he was a vagrant who sought shelter in doorways, an art gallery, and the library. These plays have nearly eliminated the moving body on stage. What connects these works is more than Beckett's minimalist aesthetic, however. In these plays and several others in his canon, the subject matter is writing, storytelling, reading, and listening as ways in which the past is remembered, reimagined, and forgotten. Acts of listening and remembering connect these plays to the audience. These plays make us aware of how much or little of what we know about ourselves is from memories we listen to or read about. Like the scene in Beckett's *Film*, in which the protagonist who is named O looks through photographs of his life–photographs that record his infancy to his present self–Beckett's characters in *Krapp's Last Tape*, *That Time*, and *Ohio Impromptu* listen to recollections of the past. Like O, they are attempting to remember and forget memories of family and love. Torn by the desire to revisit the past and by the agony of knowing that others have witnessed and are witnessing his life, O tears up a series of photographs, each from a different time in his life, after looking through all of them. Like many modernist writers before him, Beckett depicted this complex set of emotions through content and form–that is, the structures he employed reflect the content of the tale.

What is more, *Krapp's Last Tape* was the first completed stage play that Beckett initially composed in English, and, as such, it obscured the narrative often cited for his leanings towards writing in French. It would be wrong to assert that Beckett practically abandoned writing in English because he believed his native tongue restricted his creative expression. As early as 1937, Beckett wrote about his dissatisfaction with his native language to his friend Axel Kaun. This letter is written in neither English nor French, but in a grammatically imperfect German, which Beckett chose to express his early dissatisfaction with English. He began the letter simply, asking Kaun if he should write his future letters to his friend in English rather than German. In the paragraph that follows, Beckett tellingly wrote:

> It is indeed getting more and more difficult, even pointless for me to write in formal English. And more and more my language appears to me like a veil which one has to tear apart in order to get to those things (or the nothingness) lying behind it. Grammar and style! To me they seem to have become as irrelevant as a Biedermeier bathing suit or the imperturbability of a gentleman. A mask. It is to be hoped the time will come, thank God, in some circles it already has, when language is best used where it is most efficiently abused. Since we cannot dismiss it all at once, at least we do not want to leave anything undone that may contribute to its disrepute. To drill one hole after another into it until that which lurks behind, be it something or nothing, starts seeping through—I cannot imagine a higher goal for today's writer. (518)

I would like to challenge the assertion that Beckett was expressing a need to turn away from English, noting that while in 1937 he was indeed frustrated with English, by the following year Beckett alternated writing freely in English and French. Reflecting more closely on the letter, we see that it is not English, but *formal* English, with its grammatical and stylistic traps, that Beckett viewed as irrelevant to the point of being like a non-existent Biedermeier bathing suit. Beckett's reference related to Germany between 1815 and 1848, an era that turned conservatively away from the ideology of individualism and independence brought on by the French Revolution, and was mired in the cheap, decorative arts which Beckett disliked. For Beckett, writing in *formal* English was similar to the conservative politics and frivolous artistic values of the Biedermeier era—that is, outdated. Beckett wished to abuse and violate this formal, written language. Hence, his choice of which language to compose in appears to be linked explicitly to the subject matter of his creative vision and the audience for which the work was intended. For Beckett, the subject of memory, listening, and composing narratives became essentially an English language project. Perhaps still frustrated with formal English, Beckett nevertheless needed his native tongue to express this frustration, as heard in *All That Fall*, Beckett's first radio play of 1956, in which one of the central characters, a blind man by the name of Dan Rooney chides his wife Maddy for using the phrase "Never pause ... safe to haven," adding that "sometimes one would think you were struggling with a dead language" (194). Ironically, Dan's usage of "one would think" instead of "I think" is overly formal, suggesting that he, too, struggles with a no longer vibrant language. The Rooneys are not the only characters of Beckett's who struggle with language. Pozzo (*Waiting for Godot*), Hamm (*Endgame*), and Krapp (*Krapp's Last Tape*) also do, as witnessed in their attempts at storytelling and writing.

Lost in translation

Beckett's own awareness of language is noted in the very titles of his plays. If we take *Krapp's Last Tape* and his play of 1972 *Not I*, for example, we see that the English titles contain a word play that does not translate well into French or German. In *Not I*, the echo of "I" as the self and eye as the body's organ of sight is lost in the French translation *Pas moi*, and the German translation *Nicht Ich*. *Moi*, which means "I" sounds nothing like *œil*, the French for eye. Likewise, *ich* does not sound like the German word for eye, *Auge*. Despite the pun, the audience does not see an eye looking at them as they do in the opening shot of Beckett's 1964 cinematic project, *Film*. Instead, in *Not I* the audience is confronted with a character seen as a mouth (a small point placed eight feet above the stage floor and a grotesquely large hole in the television screen) and this mouth oddly refuses to use the word "I"–rejection that speaks to the mouth's refusal to *see* the story she tells as her own past. Likewise, the resonance between Krapp as the name of the protagonist in *Krapp's Last Tape*, and "crap" does not exist as clearly in modern French or German, which is perhaps why the titles of the translations are less playful. *La Dernière bande* and *Das Letzte Band* translate literary as The Last Tape.

The name Krapp makes an English-speaking audience immediately think of "crap," which brings about associations to the protagonist's constipation, as well as the suggestion that his life has become "crap" and the book he had written, at least when taking into account the number of copies sold, was also deemed "crap."[1] Julie Campbell's "The Semantic Krapp in *Krapp's Last Tape*" offers a fuller examination of this wordplay. According to Campbell, however, the word in its French form (crappe) and Dutch form (krappe and krappen) holds the meaning of last or dregs (63). Modern audiences, even those who would have seen the first productions of *Krapp's Last Tape*, are not likely to have heard those echoes. Through her exploration of the word's origin, Campbell revealed that even if the French and German audiences do not pick up on the resonance of Krapp with crappe and krappen, the play is clearly about excess and elimination. She concluded her semiotic study with the understanding that "Beckett's use of scatology," while drawing on our "shame, disgust, and morality," ultimately is directed at our "enjoyment of things anal and taboo" (69).

Campbell's insights remind me of Beckett's letter of December 29, 1957, to the American director Alan Schneider. Beckett and Schneider shared a closeness that can be witnessed in the correspondence they kept until Schneider's death in 1984. In his response to Schneider's task of writing an article on *Endgame*, Beckett wrote: "My work is a matter of fundamental sounds (no joke intended), made as fully as possible, and I accept responsibility for nothing else. If people want to have headaches among the overtones, let them. And provide their own aspirin" (82). On the surface, Beckett's response is one of the frustrated author plagued by reporters and critics. However, it provides insight despite itself. The joke, though unintended, refers to bodily sounds and, as such, makes us think of Krapp's straining to evacuate his words, much like straining to evacuate his human waste. But Beckett's response does more than align the writer's struggle to create with bodily evacuation. It speaks to his interest in listening and to the nuanced word choices and sentences that open up multiple associations for the listening audience. Beckett's choice, then, of which language to first write a play in was linked to more than merely a frustration with one or another language. It was linked to aesthetic and practical reasons.

While Beckett was by no means writing with the audience in mind—as commercial theater sometimes does—the audience was nonetheless a motivating factor when choosing the language in which to compose his plays. After *Endgame*, Beckett received numerous invitations to create plays. These invitations naturally would dictate which language the play was initially conceived in. For example, when Beckett scholar S. E. Gontarski invited him to write a play for a symposium celebrating Beckett's 75th birthday, Beckett sent him *Ohio Impromptu*. This short play is written in English and titled after the location of Gontarski's academic appointment and of the symposium, rather than after a place Beckett had visited; its text deals with the acts of reading and listening—crucial acts that academics of literature engage in. *Catastrophe*, a play that shows the rehearsal process as one in which the actor and assistant director are ordered about by a tyrannical director, had a similar genesis. It was first written in French, fitting for this 1982 play that was created at the invitation of the Association Internationale de Défense des Artistes (A.I.D.A.) for an event that brought awareness to and was protesting the mistreatment of artists and, in particular, the Czech writer and later president Vaclav Havel who was under house arrest as a result of his political leanings and experimental literary works. This is only to say that Beckett's reason for writing, the language and topics he chose, were sometimes motivated by an invitation or commission. Beckett's literary output was not always the product of pure creative inspiration; sometimes he wrote about views he was obligated to express, echoing his own 1949 assertion made in dialogue with French art critic and historian Georges Duthuit. Beckett theorized that an artist did not paint out of a need or desire to express himself: "The expression that there is nothing to express, nothing with which to express, nothing from which to express, no power to express, no desire to express, together with the obligation to express" (139).

Beckett's *Krapp's Last Tape*, *That Time*, and *Ohio Impromptu*

The focus of this chapter will be three plays—*Krapp's Last Tape*, *That Time*, and *Ohio Impromptu*—all of which explore the links between remembering and forgetting, with that of writing, reading, and listening—one of the themes that will consume Beckett's career in theater for more than two decades. This theme was often explored in English before he translated the play into French and before the work was translated into German. Perhaps his pull to compose these works in English was, in part, because they embody memories of the Ireland he left behind, and the England and France where he lived in self-exile. Seán Kennedy noted that "Again and again, reading the works written after 1946, we encounter certain Irish images—images of the father, of walking in the Dublin hills—that recur obsessively."[2] Kennedy's exploration is that of the fiction collection, *Text for Nothing*, but his analysis that "they can be read, in part, as songs of self-exile" (13) reflects the works discussed here, especially *That Time* and *Ohio Impromptu*, although Krapp, too, has exiled himself in his den. These plays depict men in self-exile striving to remember and to forget the past.[3]

Krapp, Beckett's craggy protagonist in his third stage play, has become one of the defining stage roles for older male actors. Written for Irish stage legend Patrick Magee, Krapp has also been played by John Hurt, Michael Gambon, Harold Pinter, and Barry McGovern, among other great actors. In addition to the rich subject matter and the lack of other actors to steal the show, the appeal of the role is the complexity of Krapp. Not just a 69-year-old alcoholic who nostalgically regrets his break-up with his one true love, Beckett's protagonist is a writer whose greatest accomplishment is selling only 17 copies of his book, and 11 of those copies were sold to "free circulating libraries beyond the seas," earning him less than two pounds (222). Krapp is, or perhaps was, a writer who, in his attempt to shape his material by recording his memories, or as he puts it, "separating the grain from the husks" (217), becomes blocked both in the biological sense of being constipated and in the mental sense of suffering from writer's block.

Beckett's struggle with language–the struggle to choose which language to write in and to find the right expressions which, ironically, are often archaic words and phrases as seen in his manuscript drafts–is echoed in the character of Krapp. In the earlier plays, the characters of Hamm (*Endgame*) and Pozzo (*Waiting for Godot*) are not merely ham actors, but also poor storytellers who often pick the wrong words despite attempting to choose them carefully. They ultimately create bad stories. On the recorded tapes too, Krapp is heard carefully selecting words and phrases indicated by his hesitations–a stage direction that occurs half a dozen times. These hesitations are distinctly different from Beckett's pauses and silences, other frequently used stage direction. Hesitation suggests a reluctance or uncertainty to go on, whereas a pause or silence may indicate deep thought, lost thought, or even trauma.

It seems odd for viewers of *Krapp's Last Tape* that the old man would forget words that he used years earlier. Krapp may not be going senile, as some audiences think and as Beckett's characters have been portrayed–most notably by Ian McKellen's and Patrick Stewart's geriatric Didi and Gogo. Instead, Krapp's inability to remember what specific words mean may be because words like "viduity" and "chrysolite" (220)–which are uttered after he hesitates–were not part of Krapp's active vocabulary. He delays, fishing for a word that sounds good to him at one stage of his life, but sounds pompous to the older Krapp and to Beckett's audience.

After one such hesitation in which Krapp searches for the right words, he selects the phrase "crest of the wave" but, unsure of its meaning, adds, "or thereabouts" (217).

Krapp's diction—his poor choice of words—and his inability to weave together a commercially compelling narrative are tied directly to his unwillingness to sustain a loving relationship. In a lecture presented at the University of Iowa, Beckett scholar Steven Connor, for whom recording is a pedagogical tool like the typewriter, explored the way in which the word "viduity" and the technology of the tape-recorder speak to time, memory, and the process of writing. He argued that with this word, Beckett brought together the image of weaving (cutting, splicing, and slicing) with Krapp's tape-recording, which had taken the place of his attempts to write. But through the word "viduity," which Connor pointed out comes from *viduare*, Beckett revealed that by depriving himself of love, Krapp is unable to weave a tale that will satisfy his readers (11). Indeed, another image of weaving is that of the tape-recorder spool. In Krapp's revelry in the word spool, he becomes less articulate, less able to weave together his story, his memoir. His "spooool" (216; 222) takes him back to an infantile state of language, like a small child learning how to speak. Unlike a child, however, Krapp selects needlessly complicated words at the age of 39. Both word choices show that he enjoys the sounds sometimes more than the meaning of those sounds, and as a result he wavers between sounding like a child and sounding pretentious.

The stock-taking that Krapp engages in through his taping ultimately moves him further away from being able to write, perhaps because he does not recognize that love—not sexual intimacy—is needed in order to be a literary artist. In *That Time*, too, the Listener makes up stories but these tales are ultimately dregs or wasted traces, because he lacks real intimacy with anyone. Quoting from Beckett's production notebook entry for the French and German productions of *Krapp's Last Tape*, Connor reveals that Krapp's listening to older tapes becomes a form of "mechanical masturbation": "Tape-recorder companion of his solitude.

Masturbatory agent" (9). Reduced to pleasuring himself and to pleasuring an old prostitute called Fanny, Krapp is a lonely man no longer able to write anything worthwhile. The last tape the audience sees him record is abruptly ended when he "*wrenches off*" the spool from the machine (223).

This solitude is aligned with Krapp's nostalgia. Much of his writing, the tape-recording, is about the past—the year gone by. These "P.M.s," as he calls them, are his post-mortems (218) as they will exist long after he has died. And, these recorded memories consist of endings and dead-ends—his mother's death, the end of his relationship with Bianca and, most importantly, his break-up with the unnamed woman on the lake with him. The memory of this woman in the punt on the lake is titled "Farewell to—(*he turns the page*)—love" (217). The audience only hears snippets of it, but from the fragments we are to understand that while punting on a lake, Krapp ends the relationship with the woman, expressing the futility of continuing. The woman "agreed, without opening her eyes," Krapp recalls (221). The audience learns nothing more about the relationship or the woman. Even the memory of his epiphany—a moment of revelation—on the small pier is one of endings. It did not serve as a lasting or meaningful inspiration, as it would have for James Joyce's Stephen Daedalus. The connection to Joyce's protagonist in A *Portrait of the Artist as a Young Man* should not be overlooked. Beckett's play, through the innovation of the tape-recorder and the younger Krapp's voice emanating from the machine, offers the audience a portrait of the artist as an old man as he listens to and remembers the events, including his mother's death and the end of his love affair, leading up to his epiphany, the extent of which the audience never learns. While for Joyce the moment of revelation led to an awakening that will inspire his protagonist to leave Ireland to become an artist, for Beckett it represented Krapp's missed opportunity. Krapp hurriedly fast-forwards the revelation that he, at 39 years old, thought was to be the main focus of the taped memory of the year gone by; it was, after all, a dead-end.

Each of Krapp's recordings is a telling of the past year on his birthday. He is alone with no one to toast to him. Like Krapp, both listeners in That Time and Ohio Impromptu are solitary creatures. That Time's Listener is haunted by a past love and as an old man is unloved and alone; Ohio Impromptu's Listener went into self-exile leaving behind his beloved. The theme of storytelling and deception arises after the first few pages in That Time: "making it up now one voice now another" and "making it up to keep the void out just another of those tales to keep the void from pouring in" (390). In Ohio Impromptu, the theme is apparent immediately, as an old man, Reader reads to Listener who is identified likewise as an old man, being in appearance almost identical to one another. Like Krapp, the Listeners from That Time and Ohio Impromptu tell stories to feel less alone.

Although the listeners in That Time and Ohio Impromptu are not clearly identified as "writers," as Krapp is, they can be interpreted as men of words who have become speechless. That Time, Beckett's strange play of 1974, opens with the face of an old man "about 10 feet above stage level" (388). The elderly man with "white face, long flaring white hair as seen from above outspread" (388) does not speak. Instead, he listens to memories real or made up that come to him from three distinct origins in the dark; in the script, these voices are identified as Voice A, Voice B, and Voice C. The effect suggests that he is surrounded by his memories—memories that can eventually drown him. The written script, moreover, does not follow the grammar and style conventions that Beckett distrusted in 1937. Instead, these memories, which haunt the old man, resemble an interior monologue, otherwise known as stream-of-consciousness, in the vein of Joyce's Penelope episode in Ulysses. In making the distinction between the conventions of the dramatic monologue and Beckett's dramatic interior monologues, French author Karine Germoni celebrated Beckett's ability to stage "unspoken, unacted thoughts" (137). Unlike Joyce's use of this style, Beckett's resembles traces—fragments of sentences, of images, that resemble washed-up dregs. Despite the seemingly random nature of the memories, reoccurring fragments suggest that the old man tries to pinpoint "that time," that moment or those moments that make up his identity.

A dialogue with Joyce

In these three plays, as in Lucky's soliloquy referred to by Beckett scholars as his "think" (*Waiting for Godot*), we see Beckett in dialogue with Joyce. Here, instead of parodying Joycean stream-of-consciousness style, Beckett threw into question the ability for writers after World War II to experience the Joycean epiphany. In Joyce's *A Portrait of the Artist as a Young Man*, the reader is taken through the journey of a young man as he must confront the imprisoning institutions of family, school, and church in pre-Easter Rising Ireland in order to become an artist. In Joyce, the breakthrough occurs through the protagonist's epiphany. The novel is told in the third person initially and moves towards the first person, thus reading as though the voice of the text is creating a portrait of the artist through a textual remembering of his journey as a young man up to this defining moment–the turning point. In *Krapp's Last Tape*, Beckett included a Joycean epiphany, but for Krapp this moment amounts to nothing more than words caught on tape. The 69-year-old Krapp does not even wish to remember "that memorial night in March" (220). While his younger self believed it was "what I have chiefly to record this evening, against the day when my work will be done and perhaps no place left in my memory, warm or cold, for the miracle that ... (*hesitates*) ... for the fire that set it alight," the older Krapp fast-forwards, impatiently looking for the memory of the love he cast aside too carelessly (220). *That Time's* Listener is an even older, more destitute man who once spoke of turning points, but he seems to have forgotten what they were. His portrait thus will never be complete and will never be among those whose portraits are hanging in the gallery he visits. The Listener in

Ohio Impromptu listens to a "sad tale" which will never be finished, even though at the play's conclusion Reader notes that "Nothing is left to tell" (448). *Ohio Impromptu* tricks the viewer into thinking the play ends, but ultimately its structure resembles a drawing by Dutch graphic artist M. C. Escher, in that the Reader's text reflects the life of the Listener. What is finished is not a portrait of a remarkable writer or man. Rather, the Reader closes the book to signify the death of this unremarkable, unloved man.

To see *That Time*, as Germoni did, as an interior monologue only is too limiting. Beckett reimagined the Joycean technique for the stage to examine identity, memoir, and trauma. In "'Without Solution of Continuity': Beckett's *That Time* and Traumatic Memoir," author Rhys Tranter astutely posited:

> *That Time* is preoccupied with issues of time. As a text, it draws attention to the difficulties of maintaining a grasp on any singular historical moment, accentuating confusion and dissonance. Whilst the protagonist's memories themselves appear to suggest loss, sadness, and melancholia, *That Time* also disrupts conventional lineal narratives of personal history and unsettles the coherence of the Western rational subject.(115-16)

For Rhys, the break from linear narratives to recall a historical moment (be it personal or public), is linked to trauma memoir, rather than Joyce's stream-of-consciousness style. Rhys drew on Roger Luckhurst's definition of the trauma memoir as "an incomplete and fragmentary slice of life" (117). In essence, Listener's voices attempt to create a narrative, while rejecting his own memoir. *That Time*'s Listener may be trying to figure out who he was "from Adam" (391), even though he will not use the word "I" when referring to himself. Although his memories are not trapped on magnetic strips like Krapp's are, they, too, are attempts to be less alone. These dregs, like the grammatically incorrect narrative told by Mouth in *Not I*, paint a picture of old man's life. In addition to identity, Beckett appears to have stressed the importance of place in this tale about the significance of remembering and forgetting. In each memory, a distinct place is recalled—the ruin identified as Foley's Folly, London's National Portrait Gallery, the Public Library, and the Post Office.

Voice A recalls that Listener returned to Ireland by ferry to seek out his childhood hiding place—Foley's Folly. While Tranter and another Beckett author, Audrey McMullan, have expounded on the image of the ruin, both drawing on the significance of decay and decomposition, neither notes that a "folly" may also mean a man-made, mock ruin, often in a large park. If Beckett meant for us to understand the ruin as man-made, he scoffed at the image of returning to Ireland and the wilds of childhood. The journey, like that of Joyce's Gabriel from "The Dead," is one of failure and inauthenticity. The focus on a fabricated ruin, links to the other places of free culture. For Beckett, Ireland was not the "home of ancient idealism," as it was for W.B. Yeats and another Irish dramatist, Lady Gregory, as seen in her book, *Our Irish Theatre* (402). What is more, England, while full of places of art and culture (manufactured objects of beauty), was unkind, ready to expel those in need of warmth. For Beckett, these cultural spaces spoke of death, or, as represented at the end of the play, dust: "whole place suddenly full of dust when you opened your eyes from floor to ceiling nothing only dust and not a sound only what was it it said come and gone was that it something like that come and gone come and gone no one come and gone in no time gone in no time" (395).

A crucial point in *That Time* is denoted by the opening of Listener's eyes midway through the play. Before this occurs, the memory of voice B says:

> hard to believe harder and harder to believe you ever told anyone you loved them or anyone you till just one of those things you kept making up to keep the void out just another of those old tales to keep the void from pouring in on top of you the shroud (390)

The voice brings up an interesting unresolved tension in the play.

Is it the memory of love that is often recalled during the 20-minute running time of this work real, or is the memory just another one of the "old tales" Listener made up to keep himself from his solitude? Voice B recalls that Listener in *That Time* once sat with a woman and, as they gazed before them, they vowed that they loved each other. Beckett described those vows as "just a murmur not touching" (388, 389, 390). The unnamed woman who sits with Listener much like the "dear one" never named in *Ohio Impromptu*, remains somewhat aloof; the image of lovers is one that does not include the tactile sensations normally shared among couples. The lovers do not even look at one another, begging the question: What type of love is this? Listener, more than Krapp, is destitute and alone. While Fanny drops by for a sexual encounter in *Krapp's Last Tape*, and Nagg and Nell in *Endgame* reminisce and even attempt to kiss one another, Listener is a "drooling" vagrant (393), muttering to himself—the type of man that most people do not see or, when they do, they turn away from such a destitute individual. The eyes of passers-by, Voice C recalls, pass over him. Krapp, too, finds that others are indifferent and, in some cases, hostile to him. He recalls admiring the beauty of a nursemaid: "Whenever I looked in her direction she had her eyes on me. And yet when I was bold enough to speak to her—not having been introduced—she threatened to call a policeman. As if I had designs on her virtue!" (219-20). Krapp's recollection of rejection and Voice C's memory of being unseen reminds me of actor Wendy Salkind's observation when speaking with me about *Not I*. Beckett, she said, gave voice to voiceless, unseen, and unloved creatures (197).

While simultaneously wanting to create stories and hold conversations (something *That Time*'s Listener has done since he was a child), part of Listener does not want to accept them as his own. *That Time*, Beckett revealed to James Knowlson, Ruby Cohn and others, is "the brother of *Not I*," another play about rejecting one's life story (531). Like Mouth, the voice designated as C reveals that the old man attempts to deny that his lived life is his alone:

did you ever say I to yourself in your life come on now (*Eyes close.*) could you ever say I to yourself in your life turning-point that was a great word with you before they dried up altogether always having turning-points and never but the one the first and last that time curled up worm in slime when they lugged you out and wiped you off and straightened you up never another after that never looked back after that was that the time or was that another time (390)

Listening to memories of his past, the old man does not, unlike Krapp, have the luxury of skipping memories that are unpleasant to hear. Rather, he must reinvent them or ignore them altogether, by refusing to say "I." It is curious that in this moment, when Voice C reveals to Listener that he does not use the first-person pronoun, the voice also recalls that Listener often spoke of "turning-points" before words failed him. In dramatic structure, the turning point is a play's climax. In this play—a work that is completely devoid of conventional dramatic structure—there is no recognizable turning point, at least none that the viewer can identify. The concept of a turning point in trauma studies is similar to the concept in dramatic structure; it leads to the recognition of the traumatic event and brings the subject on the road to recovery—a resolution to the traumatic event haunting the individual. In Beckett's play, Listener never confronts his trauma and thus his memoir is doomed to continue in a repetitive "downward spiral"—a phrase used by the American director, Xerxes Mehta (378). Listener's memories will keep haunting him. Even more curious is the image that follows—that of a slimy curled-up creature. It is, on the one hand, an image of birth—before a baby is wiped clean of the mother's placenta. On the other hand, the image is one of destitution, much like the images of Moran in the novel *Molloy*, who has lost his ability to walk and of Woburn in the radio play *Cascando*, both characters winding up crawling in the mud.

The common thread: love

One memory that recurs in all three plays is that of love. Yet, unlike Krapp, it is unclear what happened to the lover in *That Time*, or if she even existed. We do not know whether it is imagined or if the love dried up like the words. All of Beckett's old listeners are lonely. In *Krapp's Last Tape*, the audience sees Krapp in his dark den alone on his birthday. Moreover, we hear how Krapp forsook love for his creative impulse to write. As Beckett pointed out, in Krapp's decisive rejection, he deprived himself of love, essentially throwing away his muse. In *That Time*, the protagonist is also without love; he imagines love, perhaps keeping himself from actual love. Beckett's commentary on his own artistic statement of striving towards "impotence and ignorance," as published in the *New York Times*, is important to understanding *Krapp's Last Tape* and *That Time*. Their world is defined by a failure to know and to create new life and work, despite Krapp's sexual appetite and ability to please Fanny, the "Bony old ghost of a whore" (222) who is astonished that he can still sexually perform. Krapp may still be able to rise to the occasion, but since he broke off his relationship with the woman in the punt, he is utterly alone. Listener in *That Time* is accused of making up a story of love in order to be less alone. He too is impotent—an old man whose "fear of ejection" (and, perhaps fear of rejection and erection as well) and his "loathsome" appearance (394) render him without the ability to complete his tales; instead, he repeats them. Hence, impotence is not merely the inability to have an erection or to produce biological offspring. In these plays, it becomes the inability to produce successful literary texts or stories. Without love, Krapp and Listener are unable to compose compelling narratives, much like *Not I*'s Mouth who was "spared" love (376), and is practically speechless, even though we hear a flood of sound from her lips. Beckett's male protagonists, too, are silent except for rare occasions.

Beckett further set himself apart from Joyce, of whom Beckett wrote, "There it seems much more a matter of an apotheosis of the word" (519). Years later, Beckett noted in his interview with the *New York Times* contributor Israel Shenker that Joyce is a "master of his material." *Krapp* and *That Time*'s Listener are not masters of their materials. Listener cannot order his tales as seen in his helplessness to choose whether he will listen and in the unpunctuated interior monologue of his memories. The den in which Krapp makes his tapes, albeit bare, becomes messy with banana peels dropped on the floor and then in the auditorium, and, more importantly, with the boxes and tape reels that he has attempted to use as a way to order his memories and thoughts. The audience witnesses Krapp's inability to restrain himself from excessive consumption of alcohol and bananas, and to keep his space orderly. He, as the audience sees, is not even a skilled operator of his tape-recorder—a machine he has been using for at least 40 years. Only Listener in *Ohio Impromptu* appears to have some control over the text read to him—a narrative that mirrors his own existence. The knocks he executes on the wooden table, while not words, communicate clearly to the character designated as Reader. Each time, Reader halts and rereads from the book. Actor Bill Largess, who was cast as Listener in Xerxes Mehta's remarkable production of *That Time* in 1996 and 2000, commented on the knocks during an interview in 2011. He noted that while Listener never speaks, he communicates through a complex series of knocks. The knocks, Largess discovered, cannot be of the same intensity or volume.[4] Since Beckett took away the actor's voice and face (it is not visible to the audience), the actor expresses tension, reluctance, and eagerness through the knocks alone (207).

In *Ohio Impromptu*, Beckett linked memory to written text and reading. The text Reader reads is the recollection of the end of the Listener's life, according to Largess: "Ultimately, the Reader is not only reading for the Listener's benefit or reading to the Listener, he's also reading about the Listener" (206-07). Elements, particularly the description of the man in a long, black coat and an old-fashioned hat, along with the description of Reader, a doppelgänger of

Listener, reading from the book, support this assertion. Unlike *Krapp's Last Tape* and *That Time*, reading and remembering is meant to offer Listener comfort and company, but like Krapp and *That Time*'s Listener, the face and body posture of Listener suggest loneliness and regret; what once offered comfort also brings sorrow. He, like Krapp, wishes to see the "dear face" once again (446), but is ultimately alone having set out on the Isle of Swans, like Krapp who shut himself in his den after forsaking love for his literary pursuits, and *That Time*'s Listener who returns to Ireland as a lonely vagrant. It is important to note that although *Ohio Impromptu*'s Listener is full of regret and considers returning to the mainland, he never does. The knocks and taps on the table allow Listener to return to some memories by making Reader repeat them. The knocking, although an image of control over his material, does not always produce the desired effect. In the play's end, the Reader refuses to go on, stating that "There is nothing left to tell" (448).

We learn that Reader wonders if he could return, presumably to Paris. His self-exile to the Isle of Swans is most likely a reference to Ile des Cygnes—a small artificial island on the Seine. For a French viewer, this isle conjures up multiple associations, all linked to the way it has been used from the 16th century onwards. In "Beckett's *Ohio Impromptu*: A View from the Isle of Swans," author Pierre Astier delved into this historical significance, outlining that the isle was first used as a place of debauchery and later as a cemetery for French protestants. From that point, it became a bird sanctuary, then a slaughterhouse, a place for invalids, and the home of a replica of the Statue of Liberty (336-37). Astier noted that all these resonances are themes throughout Beckett's work. As such, the reference became Beckett's "swan song," much like W. B. Yeats's "Circus Animal's Desertion"—a melancholic poem in which the Irish poet numerated his thematic content from his earlier poems.

Astier also said that the word "impromptu" is rich with meaning. He noted that it means "on the spot" (331), thus offering a joke—the work was written laboriously, as the manuscripts show, and Beckett was not present during its debut. He neither wrote it "on the spot" nor was he "on the spot"–that is, in Columbus, Ohio–for the rehearsals or performances. Moreover, Astier reminded us of other famous "impromptus," written by Molière, Jean Giraudoux, and Eugène Ionesco, all French playwrights whose works Beckett was familiar with. Their plays, however, are "satirical attacks against their respective critics" (332). Beckett's play is not, despite its references in the early drafts to the University of Reading's Archive and the Harry Ransom Collection in Austin, Texas–both institutes already held manuscripts belonging to Beckett. In spite of writing the play for scholars like Gontarski, Beckett did not attack these academics or critics who would attend the symposium. Rather, Beckett's play teased them, offering them another puzzle that Beckett refused to speak about.

"Beckett's dying remains"

There is no doubt that all three works I have discussed in this chapter deal with the end of life. *Ohio Impromptu* moves from "little is left to tell" to "nothing is left to tell" (448). Like the reference to the dust and shroud in *That Time*, in *Ohio Impromptu* Beckett employed images of death in the character Reader is essentially a ghost or shade who is sent to comfort the Listener, until the book is complete and the Reader must depart. If *Ohio Impromptu* is Beckett's swan song, then "impromptu" refers to the mid-17th century meaning of the word–"in readiness." Although there are other concepts for this word, the image of the two figures on stage resembles 17th-century Dutch men–with their long white hair, wearing quarter hats and long, black coats, suggesting that Beckett wished to draw our attention to this sense of the word. As such, we see Listener preparing for a time when nothing remains of his life–a time when no more stories can be told. Beckett was perhaps preparing his "last" play in the vein of *Krapp's last tape*. As Adam Seelig posited in his manuscript study of *Ohio Impromptu*, "Beckett reshapes the text in order to rid it of any explicitly personal accounts that appear in the initial writing as he labors to write himself out of the text" (376). Seelig pointed out that, ironically, "Beckett left behind his manuscripts as a trace of the life that went into *Ohio Impromptu*, and these defunct drafts somehow continue to draw their eternally final breaths, for they are Beckett's dying remains in which Beckett dying remains" (389). Despite this melancholy thought, Beckett's "sad tale" would not be his final play. Two more would be written in the three final years of his career and last eight years of his life. For Beckett, reading was a form of recalling a recorded memory, perhaps even allowing it to be reshaped by those reading and listening.

Krapp's Last Tape, That Time, and *Ohio Impromptu* speak to the ways the male protagonists lose their ability to remember the events that shaped their lives and, what is more, they lose the ability to translate their memory into stories that transform their lonely existence into one of authorship. These male characters, alone, elderly and, in one case homeless, repeat—in the manner that dulls and deadens the experience—remaining memories and traces. These traces, as Beckett revealed, become fainter, fizzling out as depicted by the end of *Krapp's Last Tape* in which the recorder continues after the tape reel has ended. In the silence, the audience hears, however softly, the turning of the reels and the flapping of the end of the tape. Likewise, when Reader closes the book, the last knock echoes in the empty chamber. Through his canonical work *Krapp's Last Tape* and his more obscure works like *Ohio Impromptu*, Beckett left behind a record of his own aging process, from a writer at the age of 52 to the writer at 75. These works reveal a trajectory towards the fizzling-out phase—echoing Beckett's title of his collection of short stories, *Fizzles*. By the end of his life, his works, albeit still profound, became shorter and his characters became less verbose. The last works are the remaining traces—the fizzling-out of a great playwright.

4. All That Fall, Happy Days, Footfalls, Not I: "Spared Love": The Trauma of Being Seen; the Trauma of Being Unseen

S tarting with the radio play *All That Fall*, Beckett turned his attention to writing roles for women, perhaps because he was intrigued by the implications of the male gaze, the objectified female body, and how the gaze and the body figure into history and trauma. The gaze is an essential component of theater—whether for the stage, radio, or television. Indeed, of all Beckett's fiction, only his late novella, *Ill Seen Ill Said* (1982), features an unnamed female protagonist. Despite this, the novella is written in the third person and therefore it situates the protagonist as an object of the gaze. We do not view the world of the novella through her eyes, but rather we gaze upon her. *Ill Seen Ill Said*, as such, does not veer far from the early prose, the novel *Dream of Fair to Middling Women* (1932), and the short story "First Love" (1946) which include female characters who are the object of the male protagonist's obsession or disgust.

Beckett's plays for women are distinctly different. They feature tormented and restricted female bodies, while simultaneously giving voice to these women. In Beckett's plays for women, the gaze is both a hostile confrontation and an act of witnessing. Increasingly, the body for Beckett is a vessel containing the painful dregs of past remnants. A radio play titled *All That Fall* features an elderly and overweight woman by the name of Maddy Rooney in the lead role. The audience hears the strain and effort it takes Maddy to travel to the railway station to meet her blind husband, Dan. During her journey, she is met with hostility. The people of the village judge her as being mentally unwell. The listening audience, however, is more understanding, even though we laugh and cringe at the journey, Maddy's words, and her encounters with the townspeople. We recognize that she is weighed down not merely by her body mass, but also by memories of her poor deceased daughter Minnie, along with the knowledge and personal histories of the townspeople she meets along the way. The listeners witness both her trauma and, through her, a decaying Ireland. In exploring Maddy's journey—one that she does not undertake often—as an adventure that embodies the personal and historical failures and dead-ends of the Irish, we can view this remarkably dark and funny radio play as a way in which Beckett embodied trauma in a heavy-set elderly woman.

Maddy's world is Ireland of the 1920s—an Ireland of the Free State—as is verified by the automobile her former admirer, Mr. Slocum, drives. His car, with its big balloon tires and crank, resembles the earliest automobiles in the village of Foxrock, as scholar W. H. Lyon uncovered in his fascinating essay, "Backtracking Beckett" (107). Indeed, all Beckett scholars have agreed that the setting of the radio play strikingly resembles Foxrock, Beckett's childhood home. It is also worth noting that with the exception of attending Portora Royal School in Enniskillen, Beckett left Foxrock in 1923 to attend Trinity College Dublin, suggesting the play is set in Foxrock at the time that he was preparing to leave. Beckett's letters concerning the writing of the play reveal as much. As documented in Knowlson's biography, Beckett penned a letter to the poet Nancy Cunard in which he reflected: "Never thought about Radio play technique ... but in the dead of t'other night got a nice gruesome idea full of cartwheels and dragging feet and puffing and panting which may or may not lead to something" (385). In a letter to his fellow countryman and writer Aidan Higgins, Beckett was more explicit about the location of the radio play:

> Have been asked to write a radio play for the [BBC Third Programme] and am tempted, feet dragging and breath short and cartwheels and imprecations from the Brighton Rd to Foxrock station and back, insentient old mares in foal

being welted by the cottagers and the Devil tottered in the ditch—boyhood memories. (385)

It is interesting that the writer who was so private and who worked hard to erase his personal experiences from his literary texts, was so explicit about the play's location being Foxrock and the sounds recalled from his childhood. Writing to two friends and using nearly the exact same wording suggests that at the time Beckett was consumed with memories of his childhood. As a side note, seven years later Beckett worked on an adaptation of Robert Pinget's *La Manivelle*, transforming it into *The Old Tune*, a very Irish radio play. Set in a noisy street, two elderly men meet once again after many years. Cream and Gorman are distinctly Irish, and the BBC recording cast Patrick Magee and Jack MacGowan in the roles. Both actors known for their Irish brogues were by then well-established in Beckett's stage plays. It is possible, as Knowlson suggested, that the Ireland of Beckett's youth consumed his thoughts in the 1950s and early 1960s because of the losses he suffered during the years leading up to *All That Fall*. Writing to his American publisher, Barney Rosset, shortly before completing the play, Beckett confessed that he was in a "whirl of depression" (387). This depression was in part due to the death of his brother. Frank had died of lung cancer two years earlier. With his passing, and earlier deaths of his father in 1933, his mother in 1950, and his friend and mentor James Joyce in 1941, Beckett had lost many of his ties to the Ireland of his youth, and his sorrow for the losses may have weighed heavily upon his mind. This is not to say that Beckett longed for Ireland. He had no desire to return to the island that had become conservative after it won its independence from England. That said, the loss of Frank devastated Beckett and that feeling took on a biographically dark, albeit comedic, turn in *All That Fall*.

Irish symbolism

The location of this play is marked in Beckett's memory as one of impotence, illness, and failure. What is more, this radio play is set in the aftermath of the Easter Rising in April of 1916. Maddy, I suggest, becomes the embodiment of Cathleen ni Houlihan–the old woman who represents Ireland in Eire's literary tradition–a figure who W. B. Yeats and Lady Gregory brought back to the cultural consciousness of the Irish through their plays.

Often, Cathleen transforms into a lovely queen, once men have sacrificed themselves to fight for the Irish cause. Beckett's Cathleen, however, encounters only men whose lives are defined by failure and impotence. The male characters in *All That Fall* find that their free will and capacity to act has been squashed by Maddy. The only way in which men like Mr. Slocum can attempt to assert his free will is by recklessly pushing forward and, in the process, running over a poor hen. Beckett's critique of Irish patriotism and conservatism is loud and clear; he depicted Ireland as a maddening and dying land. Dan Rooney tells us that even the attempts to bring back Gaelic as Ireland's official language has failed. Gaelic is pathetically used to label public toilets (195).

Maddy's first aural encounter is not with Christy–one of the many men she meets along the way. Rather, it is with music, namely Franz Schubert's *Death and the Maiden*, heard coming from a neighbor's house. Upon hearing the music, Maddy comments, "Poor woman. Alone in that ruinous old house" (172). Immediately, Beckett's play raises questions–some answerable and others not. We learn only that this neighbor is old and lives alone in a big house; she listens to the same record all day long but why she does this is left unknown. About Maddy we learn more. When speaking with Christy, the farmer selling dung, Maddy reveals that she is on the way to the train station to surprise her husband. Unlike the woman listening to Schubert, she has left the domestic space exposing herself in the hostile public space–the patriarchal world in which children jeer at her and her husband and neighbors pay little attention to her. We wonder whether Maddy, although old and fat, could be the maiden who meets with death?

During her journey, the listeners discover that Maddy does not regularly meet Dan at the station. But she ventures out because she does not want to be cooped up in a "ruinous old house"—a nod to the big houses of the Irish literary tradition. These novels, notably those of Maria Edgeworth, explore the decline of the Anglo-Irish, as witnessed in the decay of their estates. Bringing together both traditions, Beckett's play reveals the decline of Ireland after its independence. Maddy has left her home—as Cathleen in W. B. Yeats and Lady Gregory's 1904 play *Cathleen ni Houlihan* has—but unlike Yeats and Gregory's Cathleen, no one listens to her in Beckett's rendition. When no one speaks to Maddy, she confronts them, insisting that she is present and alive: "Do not imagine, because I am silent, that I am not present, and alive, to all that is going on" (185). Maddy is aware of her surroundings; she is a witness. She sees more than most of her fellow Irishmen and women. She is also aware of the pain she has embodied. "Do not flatter yourselves for one moment," she continues when still no one acknowledges her presence at the station, "because I hold aloof, that my sufferings have ceased" (185). Unlike the old woman who enters the home of the Gillane family and persuades the young man, Michael, to leave behind his fiancé, his dowry, and his family to fight for Ireland's freedom in Gregory and Yeats's *Cathleen ni Houlihan*, Maddy can no longer enchant the men of Ireland to even acknowledge her existence—an extension of their sufferings. Not even her former admirer, Mr. Slocum, can stand her presence for long. As Maddy knows, she is a "hysterical old hag ... destroyed with sorrow and pinning and gentility and church-going and fat and rheumatism and childlessness" (174).

The trauma she embodies most is that of the death of Minnie—most likely her and Dan's daughter. Beckett's Ireland is full of childless individuals (despite the high birthrates in the country). Christy and Mr. Slocum do not appear to have had families and Mr.

Tyler, the old bill broker, tells Maddy that his granddaughter has had a hysterectomy: "They removed everything, you know, the whole ... er ... bag of tricks. Now I am grandchildless" (174). By extension, then, Ireland is depicted as a place that lacks new and progressive ideas. Minnie, the boy who falls out of the train, and Dan's occasional desire to kill Jerry, the boy who serves as his guide, are all images of an old, childless Ireland–a country hostile to life that will not see a vital rebirth of new thought. It is a place in which priests and audiences banned and picketed J.M. Synge's masterpiece, *Playboy of the Western World* (1906), Sean O'Casey's *The Plough and the Stars* (1926), and that condemned James Joyce's *Dubliners* (1914) and *Ulysses* (1922).

That said, there are children in this radio play: the girl at the station whose mother warns her that she may be sucked under the approaching train if she stands too close to the tracks–a wink towards Winnie's predicament of being swallowed by the mound of earth in *Happy Days*, Tommy who is nearly crushed by the weight of Maddy as he helps her out of Mr. Slocum's automobile, Jerry who Dan has threatened to kill, and the Lynch twins who jeer at the Rooney's. In Beckett's works, there is nearly always the presence of a child or the mention of one. For instance, the boys who in *Waiting for Godot* and Beckett's television play *Ghost Trio*, bring only news of naught and the memories of childhood, or children in *Happy Days*, *Come and Go*, and *Not I* who live a loveless existence. For Beckett, the physical appearance or mention of children in his plays, ironically, signals distaste, disgust, and a rejection of fertility, while at the same time conveying a longing, as witnessed in the three women who have dreamt of love since they were girls in *Come and Go*. The children in *All That Fall* are no exceptions. They do not offer hope for the future. Rather, they are in constant danger and are themselves cruel. Their presence contributes to the sorrow and pining of Maddy. It is, after all, Jerry who tells Maddy about the "little child [who] fell out of the carriage" (199). The revelation at the play's conclusion results in a note of the sinister. Maddy must live with the possibility that Dan has thrown the child out of the carriage. For Knowlson and another Beckett author, John Fletcher, Dan is responsible for the boy's tragic death, but both insist that Dan may not have intended to kill the child, even though Dan's confession that he desires to harm Jerry suggests otherwise. If Dan is responsible for the child's death, the audience is invited to wonder whether he could have also been responsible for his daughter Minnie's death? The play does not answer this question; rather it leaves the audience and Maddy with the weight of Minnie's and the boy's tragedies. Beckett, thus, suggests that this new Ireland is hostile towards the young and as such is a place retarded, as the train is on its short journey.

The train is one of the most important technological advances of the modern age. Progress, such as the invention of the train and the formation of an Irish Free State in 1922, was the result of violence, leading to destruction and impotence. The violence that paved the way to the Free State took the lives of many young men—as did World War I and II. What the Irish were left with, Beckett's play suggests, was not a rejuvenated land but rather an old and weary place that has gone mad. It has driven Maddy to madness. The Lynch twins and the adults Maddy encounters treat her as if she is crazy. She even recollects, in an extraordinarily funny moment, going to see "one of those new mind doctors" concerning her "lifelong preoccupation with horses' buttocks" (195). In this radio play, Beckett displays a humorous preoccupation with posteriors. Along with the absurdity of her obsession over the tail-end of horses, this moment reflects back to Mr. Slocum, the proprietor of the racetracks and Maddy's former admirer. The sounds of shoving Maddy into his automobile come back to us, presumably by pushing her inside the vehicle from the rear. We are also transported back to Maddy's excited suggestion that Christy whelp the bottom of his hinny to get her moving again. While not a horse, a hinny is in the equine family, being the offspring of a female donkey and a male horse. Furthermore, in Maddy's remembrance of her visit with a psychologist and Mr. Slocum himself, Beckett recalled his own childhood and the racetracks that once occupied the field near the Foxrock Rail Station. Beckett deromanticized the grandeur of Ireland's past by peopling it with characters who obsess over the past–the Sunday races, the Irish language, and engineering feats like the ocean liner Lusitania, which was ultimately downed by a German U-boat in 1915.

Beckett's Ireland was robbed of its young men and no longer sane. *All That Fall* is peopled with old men, women of various ages, and a few children. There do not appear to be any men to court young women like Miss Fitt. After *All That Fall*, Beckett erased any sign of women who are of childbearing age. The only younger women who appear are those of ghosts or voices in the heads of men such as the longed-for woman who appears as a ghost in the 1976 television play *... but the clouds ...* and the voice of the former lover in the 1965 television play *Eh Joe*. They are not present in the flesh.

"Cathartic transcendence"

After *All That Fall*, Beckett wrote plays for and worked closely with actresses, most notably the British stage and screen star, Billie Whitelaw. Beckett found Whitelaw a remarkable woman to work with. Her range of voice (like Patrick Magee's) and her willingness to be under the constraints that Beckett imposed upon her (as in her famous *Not I* and *Happy Days*, both of which Beckett directed) won him over. Their professional relationship has been the subject of many articles and books. Whitelaw, in her remarkable autobiography *Billie Whitelaw ... Who He?* and in interviews, recalled the energy and pain involved in acting in Beckett's work. In 1990, she told Beckett author Linda Ben-Zvi that "Every damn play of Beckett's that I do involves some sort of physically or mentally excruciating experience" (5). To Beckett scholar Jonathan Kalb, Whitelaw revealed that with "Each play [of Beckett's] I do, I'm left a legacy or scar" (236). What she revealed in these interviews is that she experienced the after-effects of the plays long after she performed them. The physical and internalized pain that the characters go through are impressed upon the actor's body. The question I have been repeatedly asked is why actors would perform in works that are so physically demanding and often terrorizing and painful. One such actor, the late Rosemary Pountney, argued that the restrictions and challenges placed on the Beckett actor have a "cathartic effect" (185). Director Xerxes Mehta, in private conversations, also spoke to the cathartic effect that he believed actors experience. Wendy Salkind, who Mehta directed in *Not I*, related to me that Mehta told her that in pushing through, she would experience a cathartic transcendence. Salkind never did. Beckett's working relationship with Whitelaw, however, was not all torment, as seen in the photographs John Haynes took of Whitelaw and Beckett during rehearsals for *Footfalls*. It appears that Beckett and Whitelaw shared an understanding that it was crucial to give voice to the painful memories of these voiceless women, as, too, Wendy Salkind noted to me when I interviewed her.

In *Happy Days*, *Not I* and *Footfalls*, all plays in which Whitelaw starred, Beckett linked memory to the female body, exploring how physically damaging the weight of memory can be. Author Antonia Rodriguez-Gago wrote that in the early plays, "past memories are kept in various containers, dustbins in *Endgame*, tapes in *Krapp's Last Tape*, a mound in *Happy Days*, jars in *Play*." In the later works, they "are embodied through sound and repeated in the stories the [Beckett's female] characters tell" (116). Quite literally, Beckett imprisoned his storytellers, perhaps to show how their memories of the past, confine them. In these plays, Beckett fully explored the female body and its relationship to the past, rather than as containing the future in the form of pregnancy, questioning whether "happy days" did and can ever exist in a world in which we struggle to be seen and to see.

Happy Days is a two-act play that features only two characters, a husband by the name of Willie and his wife, the central character, named Winnie. Winnie, like *All That Fall's* Maddy, is a childless woman who seeks her husband's attention. However, unlike Maddy,

Winnie is literally stuck in a mound of earth and Willie sits behind the mound where the audience can only partially see him. Another striking difference between Winnie and Maddy is in their appearance. Although we do not see Maddy, we are told that she has lost her looks. She has aged poorly–an out-of-shape woman crippled with rheumatism. Winnie, as Beckett described, is plump, in her 50s, dresses provocatively, and is "well-preserved" (138). During the play, too, we see Winnie attempt to pretty herself, touching up her lipstick, primping herself in her tiny mirror, combing her hair, filing her nails, and putting on her hat. She has a sexual allure about her, practically absent from other female characters in Beckett's theatrical canon, and with her awareness of her appeal (even if faded), she longs for her husband's attention once again. That is, she desires for him to remark on her once golden hair rather than read his newspaper and lust over the pornographic postcard. Winnie resembles Blanche Dubois, that fated southern belle of Tennessee Williams's *A Streetcar Named Desire*. Like Blanche, she hides her shame. But unlike his American contemporary who was explicit about Blanche's fall from gentility, Beckett did not provide such clarity. Instead, he positioned the audience in a similar state of longing to know what traumatic experience haunts Winnie. Needless to say, she is a complicated character, calling out Willie's sexual desires as disgusting, despite devouring with her eyes his pornographic postcard, wanting to be looked at, and then cringing from the coarseness of the onlookers.

Winnie's mound, essentially, functions much like Maddy's body mass. In swallowing Winnie's body, it represents the painful memories Winnie embodies. The memories that trouble Winnie are both personal and historical. The personal memory seems to be that of a girl named Mildred. The name echoes *All That Fall* in Maddy's own sorrow over her daughter Milly. The name Milly is, after all, a derivative of the name Mildred. In *Happy Days*, Winnie narrates the tale of the child, Mildred who, upon leaving her bedroom, shockingly sees a mouse running up her thigh; Winnie's story is that of a child being in danger in her home, a place that should be safe. That safety is thrown into question when Mildred, like Winnie, is exposed to vermin. Winnie, out in the desert wilderness, is penetrated by an ant carrying an egg–a moment that echoes the memory of a mouse running up Mildred's thigh. Even though Winnie is not afraid of the emmet–even if the audience is–, the recollection of the mouse makes her scream. The buried memory of Mildred may be a festering trauma for Winnie which resonates for her because she is left defenseless, trapped in the mound, and with a silent partner, echoing the helplessness of the child.

The story of Mildred, author Paul Lawley compellingly argued, stands for "a sexual violation" (98). To begin with, this child, who snuck out of her room at night, undresses her new waxen doll, "Scolding her ... the while" (163). Undressing a doll is, of course, a natural curiosity for children. However, the child's scolding of the doll is not. When Winnie breaks off this story, the audience immediately is left hanging with a burning curiosity to know what happened. The audience wants to peer into this closed door to discover what keeps Winnie from continuing. Instead, Winnie calls out to her spouse, Willie, for help and when he does not respond, she goes back to the memory of a rude man who, in addition to staring at Winnie, asks his partner sexually explicit questions about Winnie. When she returns to the story of Mildred, she can no longer control her emotions. Winnie screams repeatedly as though she is Mildred, an act that suggests that Winnie suffers from a traumatic incident which she fictionalizes as Mildred's and relives both in the tale she tells and in the memory of a further violation by the stranger who asks his partner to find out if Winnie is wearing any undergarments. Winnie's recollection of his desire to know echoes Mildred's undressing of the doll. That is, the man's inquiry suggests that Winnie is the embodiment of Milly's doll. He, like Milly, wants to see what Winnie/the doll has on underneath. These references leave us to wonder whether or not her recollection of this man, who she names Mr. Shower, or Mr. Cooker, is additionally a fictionalizing of an act of sexual violation. What that traumatic event is and when it happened are left unknown. While some, including in a previous work myself, like to situate the traumatic experience in childhood, it is equally likely that it happened later.

It has often also been assumed that the recollection of Mr. Shower, or Mr. Cooker and his crude comments are events that took place whereas the story of Mildred is a fictionalized account of an event. Beckett, however, does not make clear the origins of either. Both are manifestations of Winnie pushing the memory of some unspeakable experience further from her, although the recollection of man's penetrating gaze seems closer to the event than does the story of a girl who is shocked by a mouse running towards her genitalia. Even in Winnie's attempts to distance herself from the traumatic experience by transforming the memory into stories, her history screams out through the retelling of that which she has tried to keep at a distance. In her attempt to forget an incident that shockingly resembles an act of sexual violation, the memory of it resurfaces and the wound becomes increasingly painful. The repetition of the word "screamed," as well as Winnie's screaming, are indications that she is reliving the event, but she is doing so without the clarity of an intentional process of working through her trauma.

Winnie's suffering

Beckett's plays for women merge the personal and political. Winnie appears to have suffered a personal violation, in addition to suffering from political and historical trauma. Written only five years after *All That Fall*, *Happy Days* explores the trauma Winnie suffers by aligning her with a troubled Ireland and the scars of World War II bombing on Normandy. Drawing a connection between Winnie and Cathleen ni Houlihan would be going too far; Beckett had become subtler in his depiction of the traumatized image of body, land, and nation. Regardless, he did depict the human body as a metaphor for land and nation. In this play, the dregs of a troubled Ireland are only evident in the exaggeration of the hostile, cockney man who comments on Winnie and, as seen only in the manuscript's draft version of the newspaper articles that Willie reads. Mr. Shower, or Mr. Cooker, the man who Winnie recalls gawking at her, may represent England's hostile relations with Ireland, but other than the words Winnie says he spoke, he has no power of his own. The Northern Ireland of the 1960s signifies a time of troubles in which the Irish Republican Army and the English military were often in conflict with one another. Could the landscape Winnie finds herself in, reflect the recent bombing and rioting that were occurring in Northern Ireland? If so, it is not the coarse English fellow who is the real danger now; rather, it is the shadow that he, as a representation of England, has cast in modern Northern Ireland and the Republic of Ireland that has resulted in the devastated spaces of Belfast and Derry. Mr. Shower, or Mr. Cooker is not a member of the aristocracy or the British government; he is a passerby, but one who represents the cruel and cruder side of England—a "coarse fellow" (156) in Winnie's estimation.

The names Shower and Cooker also reflect Germany's destructive approach to their enemies. As has been pointed out by Ruby Cohn, the names eerily sound like the German words, *schauen* (for Shower) and *kucken* (for Cooker), both meaning to look and gawk at (182), thus representing the hostile gaze, while Winnie's reflections represent acts of witnessing. A further association that Cohn misses is that the Nazis gassed Jewish people and others who were identified as undesirable and expendable literally in showers, and thereby burned the bodies of their victims. Mr. Shower or Mr. Cooker, then represents a force that threatens Winnie's very existence. In the manuscript draft of *Happy Days* the items in the newspaper Willie reads provide insight into the way World War II still occupied Beckett's thoughts. As reported by Beckett scholar, Gontarski, Beckett wrote: "Rocket strikes Pomona, seven hundred thousand missing" and "Rocket strikes Man, one female lavatory attendant spared" (80). The story from the yellowing newspaper that by far incites the most laughs is the one pertaining specifically to Ireland: "Aberrant rocket strikes Erin, eighty-three priests survive"

(80). In Beckett's draft of *Happy Days*, Ireland suffers, too, from war destruction. The reference to the priests pokes fun at Catholic Ireland and its assumptions that staying out of World War II has kept its citizens safe. Perhaps there is more behind this joke, though. It is known that Gloria SMH, the cell of the Resistance Beckett was involved with, was betrayed by one of its members, a Catholic priest. It is possible that Beckett was criticizing the priest's betrayal, a problematic position that kept this clergyman and the Catholic Church safe. Likewise, Ireland's neutrality kept the island from being physically scarred by bombs. Its neutrality, however, was less about keeping its inhabitants safe than it was a stand against England and in agreement, at least partially, with fascism. Although no physical harm has met the Irish priests and the church in Beckett's early version of the play, Ireland, for Beckett, became a wasteland, much like the barren space depicted in *Happy Days*.

Happy Days testifies to Beckett's involvement with the Irish Red Cross in their post-World War II efforts to assist the Allies. The reconstruction of Saint-Lô and Beckett's involvement in those efforts, are recorded in Phyllis Gaffney's extraordinary book, *Healing Amid the Ruins: The Irish Hospital at Saint-Lô* (1945-46). In the book, she recalled "the real experience of a Saint-Lô citizen who was found by rescue-workers standing upright, unable to move, stuck in the ruins of his house" and the strange sight of "the women of the town, who would emerge into the sunlight from their dusty cellars, beautifully turned out in starched white blouses" (76). Such memories, which Gaffney collected from letters and photographs, including those from her father, Dr. James Gaffney, journals, newspaper clippings, and more, reminded Gaffney of Winnie in *Happy Days*. The play's desert wilderness eerily resembles the obliterated streets of Saint-Lô, reminding us that bombs can wipe out all visual clues to a city's infrastructure. Winnie reveals that Mr. Shower, or Mr. Cooker, and his partner were the last humans to pass by, echoing the destitution found in *Endgame*. She, however, is out in the hostile public and patriarchal world, whereas Hamm and Clov are in the less unfriendly domestic world. In *Endgame* and *All*

That Fall, the hostile patriarchal world is one in which women and children are in grave danger.

Footfalls, Rockaby, and *Not I*

In *Footfalls* and *Rockaby*, Beckett moved his female protagonists inside. No longer the object of the male gaze, these women exist in a hostile, lonely world. Plot summaries are helpful here before delving into our discussion of these two obscure plays. In *Footfalls* (1975), a short play with a running time of less than 30 minutes, the character May is seen pacing on stage. In the first scene, she and her mother converse. Her mother, designated as a voice offstage, is never seen by the audience. Their dialogue reveals that May takes care of her elderly and ill mother, and her mother reveals that May's pacing is compulsive. In the second scene, May's mother shares with the audience the lonely and isolated life May has lived. The audience sees May pacing, while May remains silent. The voice of May's mother is silent in the third scene. May paces and tells a story about a mother who she names Mrs. Winter and her daughter Amy. The fourth scene, just an empty stage, suggests that both mother and daughter are no longer alive.

In *Rockaby*, too, Beckett created a mother-daughter dynamic. However, in this play from 1980, Beckett's unnamed protagonist is seen rocking in a chair, while a voice off stage poetically shares with the viewers that the woman, like her mother, is alone in her home. Each time the voice pauses, the woman asks for more. The rocking chair, meant to be a comfort, lulling her to sleep, serves as a reminder of her and her mother's lonely ends.

The strangest of these late plays, *Not I* (1972), was written for two actors but only one speaking part, depicts a woman who is narrating her loveless life from birth to her present old age. She recalls being abandoned by her parents, growing up in an orphanage, and being in court for some unknown crime. In the monologue spoken at a feverish pace, the woman, who is not named, reveals that she is normally silent except on rare occasions. This is one of those occasions. Despite the need to talk, this character refuses to use the pronoun "I" when telling her story. This woman, the audience discovers, hears a voice in her mind that attempts to tell her that the story she tells is the story of her life. As if the play's monologue is not challenging enough, the actor stands on a platform to elevate her and is draped and lit in a manner in which the audience only sees her mouth. The supporting role is that of a draped man or woman, the gender being unimportant for Beckett. This character paces at specified times and raises her or his arms in a gesture to express "helpless compassion" (375).

Beckett's women should find comfort in their rocking chairs and in the light of their homes, but instead they find themselves plagued with memories of a loveless existence.[1] Unlike Gogo and Didi, Nagg and Nell, Krapp, and Winnie, creatures who had experienced love, May in Footfalls, the woman in Rockaby, and the Mouth of Not I have had, as Beckett ironically put it in Not I, "no love ... spared that" (376). The elderly women in these late plays, as such, are left alone, suffering in isolation from events that have caused them great trauma. Their "mothers" are not present in the flesh, nor is there a presence of any children. The characters in Beckett's 1975 play Footfalls and 1972 play Not I recall interactions that remind one of Maddy's journey to the railway station in All That Fall. While May's journey is much more restrained than Maddy's, the audience recognizes that in her pacing up and down the strip of light she is retracing some event or experience in her mind. She is physically and mentally pacing but what it is that sets her on this journey inward is unknown. Is she like the woman in a ruinous old home in All That Fall, unable and unwilling to face the world outside? The only time we get a glimpse of that world beyond her current space is in her memories of church. Another intersection between Maddy and May is the play's awareness of the body and gaze. Unlike Maddy, who we are told is a heavyset woman, May is "a tangle of tatters" (402)—so thin that hearing her feet shuffle is not an easy task. Both are opposite extremes of what is deemed attractive, yet both seem to need and feel tormented by the gaze, the patriarchy's engrained confirmation of a woman's worth. While May does not insist on interacting with people outside her home, she shuffles her feet, as she needs to "hear her feet however faint they fall" (401) to know she is alive. Her existence, however, is troubling to her. Interestingly, her exchanges with her mother are defamiliarized in that the actor who plays the mother is situated beyond the stage and thus out of the audience's sight. May and her mother never share the same space on stage, suggesting that perhaps, too, her mother's presence is in her mind. What is more, in a dialogue May creates between Amy and Mrs. Winter (at this point, May speaks for both characters), May essentially denies her own existence as well as her mother's. In having May recall this particular Sunday in church by renaming herself Amy and her mother Mrs. Winter, Beckett portrayed another character's attempt to distance herself from the experiences that result in her trauma.

It is interesting that in all the plays in which Beckett features women, and some in which he features men, the protagonist tells a story in the third person of an incident that most likely happened to her. In Winnie's recollection of the story of Mildred as one that happened to someone else, in May's story of Mrs. Winter and Amy, as well as in her story of pacing the aisle with a man, and in the most extreme version in Mouth's frantic story of the life of an unnamed woman referred to as "she," Beckett depicted these women as unable to face their past. The personal histories of these characters are painful; they are tales that result in trauma. May appears to be stuck between reliving her traumatic experience in her mind and rejecting it as hers; she lives in a ghostly state—a state of limbo. As such, the audience comprehends little of what may be her trauma. We know that since girlhood she has rarely left home. Now in her 40s—if we believe the voice of her mother—she has become an old, childless woman. The viewer is left asking the following questions: Could the trauma that she suffered be linked to the church, to the man who led her up and down the aisle? Or is May one of those unfortunate women left unmarried to care for her aging mother—a popular theme in the visual and performing arts, including in Tennessee Williams's *A Streetcar Named Desire*, Martin McDonagh's *The Beauty Queen of Leenane*, and contemporary movies like *Hello, My Name is Doris*.

Curiously, the place outside the home that is recalled is church. The family home and church, two strong Irish institutions which James Joyce attacked in his fiction, resonate with Beckett's interest in the work of Bishop George Berkeley, the 17th-century philosopher whose "esse es percipi" finds its way into several of Beckett's stage and television plays, and is directly quoted in the screenplay of *Film*. For Bishop Berkeley, existence was defined by being seen by God. Indeed, religion and mythology are ways for human beings to understand that which is ultimately unknowable and perhaps even incompressible. We understand humankind in terms of our religious texts and myths. As a survivor of the atrocities of World War II and an atheist, Beckett found Bishop Berkeley's emphasis on sight as central to existential crises. Despite May's devotion to church-going and Beckett's capitalization of the pronoun "he" in May's recollection, May is not assured that she exists. For her, religion does not answer the question of Being. The voice of her mother cannot likewise confirm that May was born. Instead, May's mother stops herself, pauses, and then continues with "The same where she began," repeating in the two sentences that follow the same word, as if to drive the point home: "Where it began. [*Pause.*] It all began" (401). For Beckett, the institution of the church cast a hostile gaze upon its parishioners. For May, it does not answer existential questions, nor does it offer a safe place where she can let go of her trauma. Under the gaze of the church, May disappears. The gaze of a merciful God that defined existence for Bishop Berkeley is put on trial in Beckett's 1972 play *Not I*.

Not I, "a universal tragedy"

Despite the bleakness of the set, Not I is another one of Beckett's Irish plays—the character who Beckett named Mouth recalls being conceived in Croker's Acres, a reference to a field near Foxrock by the same name. Boss Croker, an Irishman from Cork, made his fortune in America after emigrating to the New World just before the Irish Potato Famine in the mid-19th century. Upon returning to Ireland a wealthy man, Croker established himself as a successful horse trainer. He kept and trained his horses in a field that was named after him. Croker's Acres is only a short distance from Beckett's family home in Foxrock. As author Eoin O'Brien noted in The Beckett Country, the reference to Croker's Acres sets up Mouth's conception and birth as events that occurred in the calm countryside (49), juxtaposing the serenity of the pastoral with the hostile event of the sexual encounter between her parents and the unfriendly world that sets her on her frenzied monologue. Adding to O'Brien's observation, in naming Croker's Acres, Beckett created a continuity he began with All That Fall in which women are navigating an antagonistic world in seemingly safe spaces. Mouth's father, unknown to her, appears to have been connected to the grandeur of Boss Croker's estate, Glencairn. Her conception, like that of the Old Man's in W. B. Yeats's Purgatory, is as cold as the breeding of horses.

Yeats's play, a devastatingly bleak look at what happens when members of the nobility marry beneath them, is echoed in this and other plays by Beckett. The set of a stone and ravished tree is nearly identical to Waiting for Godot. In Purgatory, the old tramp who begat a son in a loveless union in a ditch, is the offspring of his mother's union with "a groom in a training stable" (30). While the tramp admits that his mother fell in love at first sight, her marriage to the stable-hand ended with her giving birth. For the tramp, the death of his mother and the status of their home occurs with the conception on a drunken night. Beckett's play does not have the same political implications and nihilism as Yeats's has. Instead, Beckett's Mouth stands in for many in Ireland and elsewhere, who live without existing. The trauma of being born, especially into a loveless world (for Yeats this is linked to the decline of good breeding), takes center stage.

Only in the monologue, spoken by Mouth at breakneck speed do we recognize that the Irish institution of family, church, and the law are once again in question. In this way, Beckett paid homage to his mentor Joyce. However, in the delivery of the monologue and the startling image of a mouth suspended in midair, as well as a second character cloaked to hide his/her gender, Beckett created a more universal tragedy than Yeats or Joyce. The tragedy is of refusing to look at the cause of human suffering; this distancing works much like Mouth's refusal to say "I." Mouth's rejection of her story is also a refusal of her embodied memories. Beckett went to the extreme in Not I in which the protagonist, like Winnie, has been swallowed up by her trauma. In the play's monologue, Mouth reveals that she is conceived and born without love, abandoned by her father at conception and by her mother at birth. She is raised in an orphanage—a home run by a religious order that attempts to teach her that God is merciful. Regardless of the speed of delivery which leaves little room for the actor to provide emotional responses to the words (nor is the actor supposed to, except in specified parts of the monologue), Mouth twice confronts religious faith, specifically the concept of God's mercy, with "brief laughter" (377), revealing the absurdity in being raised to believe in a merciful God as the waifs in the orphanage were. Mouth's trauma of having been born into a loveless world manifests itself in the mad stuff that speaks of her adult troubles. For example, we know that she had some legal problems, as she recounts being in court, but what crime she is accused of is never revealed. The specifics we desire are buried in the darkness with the rest of Mouth's body; they remain unspoken, as Mouth remains speechless for most of her life. In spite of the lack of information we are given, the play's second and silent character, who is referred to in the script as auditor, makes gestures of "helpless compassion" (375). It is unclear, however, if the auditor truly leads the audience to feel the same as he/she does.

While Not I and Footfalls do not specifically point us to historical events that had deep psychological impact for the characters–the painful past of these creatures is personal but not unusual–the portrayal of silence, the unspeakable, attests to trauma studies. What is fascinating, furthermore, is that the personal and shared trauma for the female characters of most of Beckett's plays can be defined by sexual absence or sexual assault, and thus the experiences Beckett's creatures relive make love questionable. Winnie's painful Mildred story, a tale that may be about molestation, and Mouth's story of her conception, which may be about rape, are particularly painful for contemporary audiences. In Writing History, Writing Trauma, Dominick LaCapra, an expert in the ways trauma manifests itself in writing, identified Beckett's plays as "a writing of terrorized disempowerment" which are "as close as possible to the experience of traumatized victims without presuming to be identical to it" (105-06). Indeed, the female characters on Beckett's stage represent traumatized and disempowered figures. However, in the strangeness of the images, Beckett provided the audience with a safety net–way to remind us that what we see is not identical to what is real. Crucial to Beckett was the gaze; the way in which we are drawn to spotlighting victims. Beckett showed us a gaze that is brutal and coarse–a gaze that rejects love.

Coming to terms with trauma

For Beckett, part of the trauma is the way in which victims are exposed. The world we live in floods us with images of psychological scars. These wounds are open for all to see and pour salt on. LaCapra, in an interview for The World Holocaust Remembrance Center, also known as Yad Vashem, explained that "more experimental, nonredemptive narratives" such as Not I, "are narratives that are trying to come to terms with trauma in a post-traumatic context, in ways that involve both acting out and working through" (179). If we accept LaCapra's analysis, then Beckett's plays, ultimately, revolve around the tension between remembering and forgetting, telling, and silencing an unknowable traumatic event. Trauma is closely linked to the failure to come to terms with the event. It is, as LaCapra theorized, an involuntary acting out of the past that has been unsuccessfully integrated into one's history. Those suffering from trauma, LaCapra explained, are "performatively caught up in the compulsive repetition of traumatic scenes—scenes in which the past returns and the future is blocked or fatalistically caught up in a melancholic feedback loop" (21). Repetition is characteristic of trauma, with the repressed experiences resurfacing and haunting the individual. The painful experiences become increasingly acted out in Beckett's plays; his characters lose speech but revolve, pacing around the danger zones of their minds, as we will see in the next chapter.

5. Acts without words: Avoiding the danger zone in Beckett's *Act Without Words I*, *Act Without Words II*, *Film*, *Quad*, and *What Where*

Beckett's last plays, whether for the stage, film, or television, have puzzled many viewers. Short and with little or no dialogue, they appear, on the page at least, to be un-dramatic, geometrical works so unlike any stage plays by his contemporaries. It is this very "silence"–the absence of plot or story, in some cases–that makes them so difficult to watch and comprehend. The focus of this chapter will culminate in a discussion of Beckett's often neglected, wordless plays–Act Without Words I, Act Without Words II, Film, Nacht und Träume, Quad, and What Where. These works reveal Beckett's interest in art, dance, and movement, as well as highlight his nostalgic look back at earlier art forms. What these innovative plays offer to the Beckett audience are aesthetic experiences that experiment with movement and motivation, as witnessed in Acts Without Words I and Acts Without Words II, and an interest in trauma which encompasses questions of intentional motivation and unconscious movement toward an unspeakable wound–becoming, even for the writer, an unknowable danger zone as seen in Quad and What Where. Trauma ultimately contains with it a quality of "looking back," an aesthetic that Beckett embraced.

Despite being conceived of as an artist whose work forges the way towards innovation, Beckett's own taste in music and art was in part, but not exclusively, that of an earlier time. His appreciation for Ludwig van Beethoven, Franz Schubert, and Robert Schumann is evident in his radio play *All That Fall*, and later his television plays *Ghost Trio* and *Nacht und Träume*; these works incorporate the music of the German composers. And, as Knowlson pointed out in *Images of Beckett*, Beckett's interest in paintings from Michelangelo Merisi da Caravaggio to Rembrandt is seen in the lighting and stage tableaus of plays, such as *Ohio Impromptu*, *Not I*, and *Footfalls*. In his handsome book that includes John Haynes's photographs of Beckett's plays, Knowlson noted that, according to Beckett's friend, the Israeli artist Avigdor Arika, Beckett's "main love throughout his life remained the work of the Old Masters" (57). Knowlson took a biographical look at the works that Beckett saw and Beckett's stage images. He concluded that "if it were possible to take X-ray pictures of Beckett's stage images, they would reveal some of the ghost-like figures of the Old Masters that have inspired visual elements in his plays" (72). For Knowlson, then, Beckett's plays are constructed as though they are an additional layer to that of earlier art forms. Knowlson viewed paintings such as Pieter Brueghel the Elder's *The Parable of the Blind*, Antonello da Messina's *The Virgin of the Annunciation*, Rembrandt's *Portrait of Jacobs Trip*, Caravaggio's *The Beheading of St John the Baptist*, and Caspar David Friedrich's *Two Men Observing the Moon*, as depicting "ghost-like figures," a description that eerily defines the characters found in Beckett's late plays for the stage and screen. His characters, often draped in shades of gray, haunt the spaces they occupy. They pace the premises or stay seated, deep in thought for those no longer present.

Author David Lloyd took Knowlson's suggestions further. Instead of focusing his discussion of the Old Masters, Lloyd looked at the very artists that Beckett personally knew and wrote about. His discussion of Beckett's intellectual and personal relationships with the Irish painter Jack B. Yeats, the Dutch painter Bram van Velde, and Arikha reveal new insight into how these artists helped Beckett to reimagine a theater that moves beyond representation of life. His theater is not meant to mirror life, Lloyd argued, but rather that "Beckett's long-standing concern with the reification or thingliness of the late-modern subject, and with painting and theatre alike as media that stage this conception of the human reduced to the condition of a thing" (21). He challenged Beckett's pessimism, stating that "it is impossible to view Beckett as anything other than a profoundly ethical writer" (21). Indeed, it is not that Beckett's silent plays remove the human condition. They reduce the human and the human condition to a thing—an essential object. Lloyd saw Beckett's work opening up the possibility to move us towards community that is "founded not on sovereignty of the subject over its objects but in the insistence of the human as a thing beyond representation, suspended in its relation to the things among which it dwells" (22). For Lloyd, Beckett's work challenged authority, as it levels all things—human and non-human—as objects. Lloyd's astute analysis is, nonetheless, difficult for the audience to grasp. When we watch bodies on stage and to a lesser extent on screen, our eyes consume bodies which we translate into subjects with or without free will, or subjects who struggle to have some sense of individuality. Beckett's work, particularly these last plays, strike us as strange. Although it is not immediately evident, this estrangement occurs because Beckett's characters are reduced to just another thing on stage; the character is an object that is acted upon.

Act Without Words I and II

Beckett's mimes of the mid-50s will help to see how he repositioned the human body on stage. Both Act Without Words I and Act Without Words II were written in 1956. The first was performed at the Royal Court in London in 1957 and the second at the Institute of Contemporary Arts in London in 1960. The first work opens with an image that would resemble Happy Days: "Desert. Dazzling light" (203). In the bare desert landscape of this mime, a palm tree, scissors, and pitcher of water descend mysteriously onto the set. A man, who is flung onto the set, trims his nails, sits under the palm, and repeatedly attempts to reach for the carafe of water. It moves out of his reach each time until the man gives up trying. Beckett peppered the mime with repetition—both in the movement and in the text. Unlike poor Winnie in *Happy Days*, the character of this mime repeatedly falls after being flung out onto the stage, but despite being pushed onto the stage and falling to the ground, the protagonist picks himself up. Each time he gets up and before he tries to get hold of the carafe dangling from the ceiling, he "hesitates, thinks better of it" and that he "reflects."[1] Beckett's descriptions reveal that the protagonist is a conscious entity rather than a marionette which acts without thought.[2] His reflections are tied to motivation—a key element in acting. An actor must not just move; he must discover why he must move. Acting instructors often ask their students to consider what the character is after. Yet the menacing nature of Beckett's mime—that is the forces that keep thrusting the protagonist on stage and that keep moving the carafe out of reach—gets the better of the protagonist. In this short work, we have the opposite of Beckett's play *Catastrophe* in which the Protagonist raises his head, as Beckett told James Knowlson, to resist the menacing Director (597). In *Act Without Words I*, Beckett shows us a man who gives up trying to fail. When he reaches his breaking point, the protagonist lies on the floor, "his face towards auditorium" (206). The fact that we are confronted with his defeated expression gives us pause. This modern-day Sisyphus no longer partakes in the futile drudgery of life, as represented in the carafe of water. What is more, the mime reveals that the human in the play is not independent from the things that dangle in front of him. He cannot exist without water or without shade. And, water and shade cannot exist without him. Eventually, when the man is reduced to a thing, motionless on the ground with no more will to go on, the other objects that once tempted him become still and lifeless.

The unknown, menacing force in *Act Without Words I*, and the reduction of the persons to things are also found in *Act Without Words II*. The first indication of this is in the description of the lighting; the stage is "violently lit" (209), much like the lighting of

Act Without Words I and *Happy Days*. From the onset, all three plays reveal that the environment that these characters reside in is violent and harsh, bearing down on the protagonists. How each of these characters responds to their environment is also similar. Each seems to respond through repetition and habit. Although the protagonist in the first mime repeatedly strives to reach for water, the protagonists in the second, like Winnie who holds on to her old ways, awaken after a jab from a goad (similar to Winnie's alarm clock) and begin their daily habits of saying prayers, dressing, and carrying the other protagonist who is inside the sack to the other end of the stage, before undressing and enveloping themselves in a sack. Both men wear the same clothes, but their temperament in carrying out their day is different. While one embraces the new day with cheer, the other drags himself through it. In this second mime, we find Beckett exploring movement and motivation, exploring the different ways in which one responds to a world beating us down and goading us to go on.

Fascinating in this second mime is to see how each man is carried inside a sack by the other. They are reduced to the things they carry around with them. The sack should contain things that the carrier needs to have with him; he is, at first glance, a hobo traveler who has a bundle containing necessary objects with him. One could analyze *Acts Without Words II* as staging existence as a routine in which we carry with us various versions of ourselves. Identity is not an expression of independence or individuality, but rather, Beckett seems to suggest, a compilation of the things we drag about with us, which emerge from time to time. In the mime, there are only two versions of the same man (similar to *Ohio Impromptu*), suggesting a bipolar representation of humankind.

Film and *Quad*

Beckett created worlds of silence, especially on screen but, it is interesting to note, this silence is not the solitude Beckett longed for in his own life, as Knowlson recalled (4). The silence in Beckett's plays is often threatening and despairing, and as such, propels some of his characters to speak uncontrollably. Beckett's short adventure into cinematic arts culminated in *Film*–a silent movie starring Buster Keaton. Yet, Beckett's dip into motion pictures occurred in the 1960s. *Film* reveals Beckett's interest in the medium which dates back to his childhood when he was taken to the cinema to watch gems of the silent movie era.[3] In 1936, the struggling writer wrote to the Russian film director Sergei Eisenstein looking to be taken on as a pupil to learn the editing and scenario writing aspects of cinema. Even at the dawn of sound film, Beckett sought direction from Eisenstein, a master of the silent film, as *Battleship Potemkin* demonstrates. Eisenstein did not respond to Beckett's letter; the reason for his silence is unknown. What is intriguing is that nearly 30 years later, Beckett wrote a silent film in which silence is not a mere convention, as it was in the early decades of the 20th century. The film's protagonist, named O, flees the cameraman named E in silence. E is in pursuit of him. O, who is played by Keaton, is afraid of E. Other characters, the couple on the street and the elderly woman on the staircase, look horrified when their eyes meet the camera. The E, the menacing eye of the camera, attempts to capture and expose O's existence, and transform him into something more than an object. Being caught on film, this experimental work reveals, is simultaneously an act of distilling life and of proving existence. We capture things and events on film to prove that they happened. O, then, does not want the weight of his existence realized. There is danger in being seen.

Of the most frustrating of these works, *Quad*, Beckett expert Graley Herren wrote: "What exactly this ineffable gesture is meant to signify is unnamable by its performers and directors and unknowable by its critics (and probably by its author, too)" (138). Herren pointed us in the right direction. He noted the "unnamable" and "unknowable" quality of this late television play. Beckett was working towards this quality–a quality that aligns with his attempts to strive towards impotence and ignorance. Along with the traces of an older art aesthetic embedded in his plays, Beckett, as noted earlier in this book, set himself up as having a different agenda from Joyce's modernist omnipotence. Beckett's vision of literature that strives towards impotence and ignorance is a vision that brought him to a point in which there are no more words, or as the 20th-century German poet and philosopher Dieter Leisegang wrote of his own work: "Lauter letzte Worte" ("All last words.") Although it may be questionable whether Beckett's plays led to the nihilism that can be seen in Leisegang's work, Beckett's *Rockaby*, a short play from 1980, made up of a woman listening to a voice recalling her own life, concludes with the voice calling for an end:

fuck life

stop her eyes

rock her off

rock her off (442)

The very late plays depict creatures who have "nothing ... left to tell," as the Reader in *Ohio Impromptu* simply puts it (448). These plays address the silence when a writer comes to the end of his words—whether it is because his characters are *silenced* through the unspeakable traumas they suffer, or because the artist no longer is propelled by an obligation to create. *Quad* is perhaps the finest example of a theater of silence.

The "undoing" of a past: lost memories

When considering *What Where*, a play in which no answers are provided despite the torture inflicted upon the characters, and *Quad*, a television play in which the characters have no voice unless it is the shuffling of their feet, against Beckett's early and more conventional work, *Krapp's Last Tape*, the viewer discovers a pattern that runs throughout his work. *Krapp's Last Tape*, while innovative in its use of the tape-recorder, is Beckett's last play which draws on a recognizable–perhaps one could even say realistic–image, and is often considered a nostalgic play lamenting love lost. And, although *Come and Go* is much more radical than *Krapp's Last Tape*, the image of three women on a park bench, recollecting the past (even if only in fragmented sentences) is not an uncommon artistic image. We need only to think of Walker Evans's photograph of three women in bonnets on a park bench in NYC, circa 1928-30. In these works, Beckett used a character's past, or, in the language of the actor, his/ her backstory, as a means to move towards erasing the need to set up such a background. Indeed, from the first plays the audience witnesses characters correcting their stories. Needless to say, it is tempting to view the acts of correction that take place as refining the past to create a more accurate account. However, in Beckett's plays, the editing that occurs is just as often an act of redefining and erasing the backstory. His characters seek to wipe out or reimagine the past as something other than it was.

More than 20 years later, Beckett had eliminated dialogue in *Quad*, and although he returned to dialogue in *What Where*, the essential "backstory" of the event and location of that event (the what and where) is withheld, forgotten, or was never known. The play consists of four characters called Bam, Bem, Bim, and Bom. The voice of Bam is heard, narrating what appears to be a cycle of interrogation to extract information. Bam exists both as a voice heard from a small megaphone and a character who takes part in the action on stage. Each character leaves the stage to enact violence onto another character; each is unsuccessful in getting the information needed. Essentially, that which stirs the characters into taking their journey off- or on-stage nowhere in these late plays is unsaid and unknowable. Despite the "undoing" of a story or past, *Quad* and *What Where* depict a coming and going that Beckett has already established through the tapes in *Krapp's Last Tape* and the entrances and exits of Vi, Flo, and Ru in *Come and Go*. I use the term "undoing" deliberately to invoke Gontarski's manuscript study of Beckett's plays. These last plays echo what Beckett did with his manuscripts. In his drafts, Gontarski argued that Beckett wrote himself (the biographical details) out of the plays. In these last plays, Beckett kept the essentials of drama—that is, movement—but erased what sets the characters in motion. The structure of these plays exposes memory in Beckett's work as a downward spiral, a winding down of the past until all but the movement that is the result of some past is left. These plays suggest that sometimes all that remains are traces from a forgotten past.

From his very first stage works, Beckett presented characters who experience memory loss. In *Waiting for Godot*, for example, Pozzo tells the tramps that his memory is defective; Didi has difficulty remembering the song he sings at the beginning of Act II; and Gogo and Didi cannot remember if they have waited in the same place the day before. However, it is not until his third staged play, *Krapp's Last Tape*, that the theme of memory and memory loss becomes the central plot. Krapp obsessively returns to one particularly painful memory—a memory when he forsook love in order to become a writer. I will not focus on this aspect of the play as so many have already done. Rather, what puzzles me is Krapp's inability to remember the definition of the word "viduity" (219). Moreover, when he looks up the word in his large dictionary, Krapp chooses the wrong definition:

> (*Reading from dictionary.*) State—or condition—of being—or remaining—a widow—or widower. (*Looks up. Puzzled.*) Being—or remaining? ... (*Pause. He peers again at dictionary. Reading.*) "Deep weeds of viduity." ... Also of an animal, especially a bird ... the vidua or weaver-bird ... Black plumage of male. ... (*He looks up with relish.*) The vidua-bird! (219)

For a writer, even a failed writer, to forget a word he used to describe his mother's state of being a widow, when just moments before having heard the word in the context of his mother dying, is curious. When Krapp associates the word with the vidua-bird,

Beckett invited us to laugh at Krapp's rewriting of the memory: his mother was a bird while she "lay a-dying" (219). What this passage suggests is that Krapp's memory of his mother's death can be read as a traumatic moment in which only the traces of her passing remain. The event in all its details is recorded on the tape, but for the 69-year-old Krapp the details are lost. What remains is the sensation of loss, as depicted in several productions of the play when the actor playing Krapp mimes a small ball being in his hand as he hears his earlier self say: "I sat a few moments with the ball in my hand" (220).

While Krapp returns obsessively to recall his last moments of love—the love he felt for the unnamed woman he went punting with and, possibly, the love for his mother—those memories, are the grains that Krapp attempts to separate from the husks. From this almost conventional play with a clear character history (Krapp and his tapes provide a backstory for the actor and audience), Beckett intensified the theme of memory loss in his 1965 play, *Come and Go*. In this play, there are three women, whose ages are "undeterminable" (353), whose faces are shaded by their "Drab nondescript hats" (357), and whose voices are "as low as compatible with audibility. Colourless except for three 'ohs' and two lines following" (357). However, their fragmented speech provides the traces of their pasts. They have names; they remember sitting together "in the playground at Miss Wade's" (354), "dreaming of ... love" (355) and holding hands. Despite this, the crucial elements to the story—the rings that do not appear to be on their fingers, and the secrets each of them tells—are unknown to the audience and the actors. In a much earlier version of the play, called *Good Heavens*, Beckett explicitly identified the content of the whispers, as Knowlson pointed out in *Frescoes of the Skull*. In the final version of the play, Beckett omitted lines that contained a story in favor of the whispers that are not decipherable. In other words, Beckett erased their secrets in favor of silence. The secrets were known at one stage, but now these ghostly creatures appear to be in a cyclical trap, forever in motion, as the formation of their intertwined hands suggests.[4] Regardless of Beckett's erasures, this play, like *Krapp's Last Tape*, is about lost love. I venture to suggest that the audience should ask at least these two questions: Are these women recalling how they lost each other to death? Or, are they lamenting that none of them ever experienced love? Either way, the traces, the remnants of their past experiences and friendships, are gone, as the figures fade into the darkness when they exit the stage–only to reappear as ghostly women haunting a park bench.

The mimes

In 1981-2, Beckett directed *Quad*, a play he wrote for the Süddeutscher television broadcasting station. The genesis of this play is well known in Beckett circles; it makes up most of the scholarship on *Quad*. Rather than retrace these steps, I want to suggest that the television play is a two-act mime (which were re-titled for the German viewing audience *Quadrat I* and *Quadrat II*) that is part of a larger trend in Beckett's plays for stage and screen. Of the television play, Graley Herren noted that

> The piece contains no language, no conflict, and no old scores to settle with the past. For all its optical brilliance, it remains one of Beckett's most obscure works–which is no mean boast. (124)

This play represents a work in which the figures have no backstory, as Herren posited, and yet, like Dante's damned,[5] seem unable to break from their journeys nowhere. The work, moreover, contains no faces and, unlike most mimes, the movement of the figures tells no story.

In an often-quoted letter to Alan Schneider, Beckett, in regards to *Endgame*, wrote:

> My work is a matter of fundamental sounds (no joke

intended), made as fully as possible, and I accept responsibility for nothing else. If people want to have headaches among the overtones, let them. And provide their own aspirin. (82)

Interestingly, Beckett did not argue that his works are about language or about dialogue. His word is "sounds." In *Quad*, the maddening movements of the characters is accompanied by sound. In the first part, *Quadrat I*, viewers hear the feet shuffling and the percussion instruments. In second, *Quadrat II*, we hear only the shuffling of the feet, now much slower but still pronounced. That which has set these figures in motion on their purgatorial journey is unknown. Several scholars have convincingly made the connection between *Quad* and purgatory–firstly, because the figures turn to the left like Dante's damned, and secondly, because Beckett described the second act, *Quadrat II*, as taking place 10,000 years later. More like purgatory than any other of his plays,[6] the figures cannot be released from that which has condemned them, because they do not know what sent them pacing. What is more, these figures avoid the center of the quad. That center, which Beckett referred to as the danger zone, is also a mystery. The viewers and readers are left wondering what danger are the characters avoiding?

While there is definitely a lack of dramatic material in the television play and the reason as to why the figures are set in motion is obscure, looking at this mime as an essential part of the Beckett's complete work I suggest that *Quad* is not without a past that haunts these cloaked characters. The shuffling feet remind a Beckett audience of *Footfalls*, for example, in which there is a tension between the past and how it defines May's existence. The teaser, however, is that the past in *Quad* is unknowable to the figures, the actors, (or rather ballet dancers who performed the work), and to the viewers.

Nacht und Träume and What Where

The television play that follows *Quad*, *Nacht und Träume* (*Night and Dreams*) is equally mysterious. Again, no dialogue punctures the script; movement, too, has been reduced. The two characters seen in the television play are the dreamer and his dreamt self. The repetition of the dream and the way it mirrors the undreamt self is suggestive of a cycle, an unanswered prayer, according to Herren.[7] Whether or not one is able to recognize the religious allusions which Herren saw as Veronica's cloth when watching the short, grainy image resembling the paintings of the Old Masters, *Nacht und Träume* reveals that our nights are filled with dreams, which recycle the events that propel characters to keep going, but also gulf them in silence.

Written shortly after *Quad* and *Nacht und Träume*, *What Where* (1983/4) returns to dialogue, but it is a dialogue that does not answer questions. This stage play (which two years after its premiere was transformed into a television play) is often read as a scene of political interrogation. And, although there is cause for such readings, primarily the abuse that is carried out to find out the "what" and "where" of the unknown story, to read this play as a political statement may be a mistake (one that I myself have made). Theorist Elaine Scarry, after all, reminded us that violence used in interrogation is meant not to extract information but rather to destroy communication. She wrote:

> Physical pain is language-destroying. Torture inflicts bodily pain that is itself language-destroying, but torture also mimes (objectifies in the external environment) this language–destroying capacity in its interrogation, the purpose of which is not to elicit needed information, but visibly to deconstruct the prisoner's voice. (19-20)

What is happening in *What Where* is not an attempt to "destroy language," or "to deconstruct the prisoner's voice," but rather an effort to restore language, to recall the "what" and "where" of some long-forgotten existence or trauma. However, the question arises as to whether language, that story that propelled the creatures in the play into silence, can be restored and retold.

An element in this play, often ignored, is the mime at the beginning of the play in which each character makes his appearance without an exchange of dialogue. The Voice of Bam, a distorted head in the television play and a megaphone in the stage play, announces:

First without words.

In the end Bom appears.

Reappears. (471)

What occurs next on the page is a series of stage directions. On stage and on screen, these directions are translated into a shadow play, a mime, in which these creatures enact the play before adding dialogue to the movement. It echoes the players in William Shakespeare's *Hamlet* who perform the play referred to as "The Mousetrap" once without words and then with words. The detail, especially the focus on "*head bowed*" and "*head haught*" (471), speaks to the tradition of the mime. Initially, we assume that this is only about the movement, but the detailed description requires miming to show the distinct power relations. Before any words are spoken, we know that the creature who will be the tormentor has a lofty, noble disposition. The character who has been tortured and yet continues to have no information to give has a bowed head. After the sequence, Bam announces, "Now with words" (472); the movements are identical to those of the mime. The difference lies in the attempt to get each B−m to confess to knowing either the "what" or the "where," which he does not admit to. The torture is administered off-stage until the beaten character passes out. However, the beating is clearly not an attempt to destroy language, even though the result is a continued silence.

It is possible, too, that there is only one character in this entire stage play; after all, the players are described as being "as alike as possible" with the "same long grey gown" and "same long grey hair" (469). In the television play, their identities are further merged into one with the stripping away of any individualistic markers. They are merely floating faces. If this is the case, then Bam may be flogging himself repeatedly in his attempt to remember some past event, just as Krapp tortures himself by returning to his recorded memories. Bam's attempt to remember is then an effort to work through some trauma. The failure to remember, however, keeps him incomplete (a floating head) and tortured (the trauma is acted out upon him).

While there is a temptation to suggest that there is clear progress in Beckett's plays towards silence, to do so would be a mistake. Many of Beckett's works are concerned with how traumatic events lead to a repetition and a silence, but with these works Beckett explored the topic rather than moved towards an understanding of it. After all, the characters in Ohio Impromptu, Not I, and Catastrophe clearly have backstories, while the characters in Quad and What Where do not. There is no "neatness of identification" (19) in the Beckett canon. What is more, the loss of memory is a concern in Beckett's plays as early as Waiting for Godot. Quad and What Where, in light of Beckett's plays that are centered around memories, also make up this theme. They are extreme representations of memory lost and the ways in which the characters replay the past, even without remembering it. Ultimately, these works reveal that even when the past is lost to us, our actions replay the very events we no longer remember.

6. Beckett's Legacy

Rather than speak of Beckett's last days spent in a nursing home, I choose, as Beckett did, not to end on this note. Endings are difficult and unsatisfactory. It is no surprise that post-World War II writers such as Beckett refused to provide clean endings. His works do not conclude with a resolution; they conclude with the implication of continuing, whether it is with the characters' resolve to return to the same spot or a journey still in progress. The final sentence of Molloy loops back to the beginning of the novel. Molloy begins in his mother's room, ready to write his report of how he got there. He ends the novel with, "Then I went back into the house and wrote. It is midnight. The rain is beating on the windows. It is not midnight. It is not raining" (176). The words often quoted by fans of the Irish writer are "I can't go on. I'll go on" (414). The repetition in Waiting for Godot, for example, implies that the two tramps, Gogo and Didi, will continue to wait without the satisfaction of ever meeting Godot. We know that they have met and waited for more than the two days that we see them, and the impression we leave with is that they will wait another day, and another and another. Likewise, the characters of Play (1962-1963), Footfalls (1975), and Come and Go (1965) are trapped, revolving the past in their minds. Moreover, the figures in Quad (1982), as well as the characters in Play and What Where (1983), appear to be trapped in purgatory–Dante's circle for those doomed to repeat their past sins.

What is more, Beckett's very insistence that there is no curtain call is his refusal to end–a refusal to express to the audience that what they experienced was not real, but only a play. Instead of a curtain call, in which the actors take their bows, from Endgame onwards Beckett created final tableaus. The elimination of the curtain call keeps the allusion that the play exists beyond the duration of the audiences' presence. It was his denial that Mouth in the production of Not I he directed was only Billie Whitelaw *acting* her part. Indeed, there is something lost when directors introduce a curtain call, as was done in 2017 for the Theatre for New Audience production of *Happy Days* starring Dianne Wiest. The spell is broken, too, with the introduction of talkbacks, as actress Lisa Dwan has done with her otherwise excellent *Not I*. The introduction of a curtain call or a talkback breaks the emotional knot Beckett has put us in. I am reminded of what the founder of La Mama's Repertory Theatre, Ellen Stewart, said of Sam Shepard's early plays. In the documentary film *Sam Shepard: Stalking Himself*, she reflects that Shepard ties his audience to his belt and takes them on a ride. Then at the peak of the play's emotional charge, he lets them go to ride it out on their own. The same can be said for Beckett.[1]

This inability to come to resolutions, to tidy endings, is essential to the question of legacy. Beckett's legacy—the way he and his works continue to frustrate audiences, to be discussed by academics, to inspire contemporary writers and artists, and be infused in popular culture—is astounding. Beckett's presence in the 21st century continues to be strong, particularly in the realm of academic circles. There are nearly as many articles and books written about the Irish author as there are about William Shakespeare. Conferences and other academic or educational meetings dedicated to the author continue to take place, such as the Samuel Beckett Society Annual Conference (which has as its mission to move the location through the Americas, the U.K., Europe, and Asia), the Modern Language Associations (which has dedicated panels on Beckett), the Samuel Beckett Summer School bringing scholars, theater professionals, Beckett fans, and students to Trinity College Dublin (Beckett's alma mater), the London Beckett Seminar (which has continued to meet to discuss his works outside of academic educational programs for over two decades), and the Debts and Legacies summer series that continues to bring international scholars to Oxford, England. One of the longest-running academic gatherings is the Beckett Research Seminar at the University of Reading in the U.K.

Often these academic endeavors, such as the 2016 gathering in

London for Samuel Beckett: Performance/Art/Writing, bring his plays to the public. Since *Waiting for Godot, Endgame,* and *Krapp's Last Tape* have become staples of mainstream theater, these academic gatherings sponsor the later works or adaptations of his work, such as Conor Lovett's extraordinary one-man shows in which he provides a minimalist staging of *First Love,* among other Beckett prose works, to secure their legacy. The Beckett Symposium in 2000 in Berlin and the centennial celebrations in 2006 brought theater companies from across the globe to showcase their productions of Beckett's well-known works, like *Waiting for Godot,* and lesser-known works, like *Ohio Impromptu, Come and Go,* and *Not I.*

There have been some exciting productions in recent years. Conor Lovett of Gare St Lazare has staged several of Beckett's prose work, including *Molloy* and *First Love.* Likewise, Barry McGovern's remarkable renditions of Beckett's *I'll Go On, Watt,* and *First Love* have traveled to London, Edinburgh, New York City, Los Angeles, and Sydney, among other theater hubs. The Out of Joint stage production of *All That Fall* received surprisingly good reviews. Upon entering the theater, the audience was given blindfolds, inviting them into Dan Rooney's world of sounds. Other theatrical experiments are featured at the Enniskillen International Beckett Festival and by Ireland's Pan Pan Theatre company. Beckett's legacy as a playwright goes beyond stage productions of his work. The 2001 Beckett on Film project was a sadly failed venture to bring all of Beckett's 19 plays to a general audience. The films were not screened in cinemas, as had been hoped and plan B, television screenings, were disrupted by Queen Elizabeth, the Queen Mother's death in 2002. Nonetheless, the project has provided fans and scholars a DVD collection that has become part of Beckett's legacy. Although academics have disagreed about the quality of the work, *Waiting for Godot, Endgame,* and several of the less frequently staged short plays and mimes have, as a result, become available to a wider viewing audience. The 2015 release of Ross Lipman's video essay, *Notfilm,* which is accompanied by Beckett's *Film,* not only offers an insightful documentary about the making of *Film*, but importantly has reawakened interest in Beckett's experimental film starring Buster Keaton and Beckett's only trip to America. Lipman's video essay contains never before seen footage, photographs, and even a recording of Beckett's voice, which most who did not have the fortune to meet Beckett had never heard.

In addition to the legacy that academics and theater professionals have carried forward, Beckett's minimalist aesthetic has inspired contemporary artists. A discussion of the links between Beckett and contemporary artists and filmmakers can be found in *Samuel Beckett and Contemporary Art*. The collection reveals that Beckett's aesthetics can be found in artists like Claire-Lise Holy (1938-2009), Vito Acconci (1940-2017), Stan Douglas (1960-), Dorothy Cross (1956-), and filmmakers like Steve McQueen (1969-), among others. The premise of scholars like Derval Turbidy, David Houston Jones, and Rob Reginio is that Beckett, too, was a contemporary artist. In October 2018, Arlene Shechet's "Full Steam Ahead" featured, among other public artworks in Madison Square Park in New York City, Dianne Wiest encapsulated in a stone performing an adaptation of *Happy Days*. Schechet, known for her colorful ceramics and curated ceramic shows, found new inspiration in Wiest's performance of the play at Theatre for New Audiences in Brooklyn. The impact of Beckett's 1961 play found resonance and was transferred to a public space—a space which invited anyone walking by to stop, stare, and reflect as the crude fellow Winnie calls Mr. Shower/Cooker does, continuing a legacy that comments on public art, public and private spaces, and the objectification of women.

The 1991 film *Happy Days* by the Russian director Aleksei Balabanov is a remarkably interesting minimalist work that weaves together several of Beckett's plays, including *Happy Days*, *Endgame*, and *Waiting for Godot*, as does Christopher Durang's American absurdist play of 1981, *The Actor's Nightmare*. While it is no surprise that our most important playwrights have been influenced by Beckett (for example, Harold Pinter, Sam Shepard, Will Eno, Marina Carr, Israel Horowitz, and Edward Albee), most do not directly weave Beckett's text into theirs. What is more, most of these playwrights move into a realm that is less minimalistic and more realistic in the image of the set, at least. Balabanov's aesthetic echoes Beckett's in its black and white filming, its eerie silences, and absurdist humor that speaks to the existence of Soviet-era communism. He moves away from Beckett in the final scene, in which the character who most resembles Clov enters a coffin and is set out to sea, mirroring the fate of Ishmael in Herman Melville's novel *Moby Dick*.

Beckett's imprint on contemporary music is also important to note. Philip Glass has long been associated with Beckett; his music coming in waves and cycles, a structure that recalls Beckett's break from dramatic conventions. Morton Feldman, too, has written works influenced by Beckett's literary output, as well as *Neither*, an operatic work for which Beckett provided the libretto. Gyorgy Kurtag's 2018 *Endgame* has been one of the most internationally successful recent operas. The opera, which premiered at the La Scala in Milan, has been lauded by the *New York Times* critic, Zachary Woolfe, as an "exquisite opera, a miracle of dedication, craft and care." With only four singers and very limited movement, Kurtag's opera is very much a musical version of Beckett's play. He veered from Beckett in that the characters are situated outside a dilapidated shelter rather than inside, looking out to the uninhabited earth. Catherine Laws's website, The Contemporary Music Center Ireland, is a wonderful resource for the scholar or musician working on Beckett.

Despite, or perhaps because of, Beckett's challenging aesthetics—his reworking and breaking from conventional theatrical structures, his work and his image have continued to draw attention from outside academic circles as well. As Eckhart Voigts-Virchow showed in his fun, quirky article in *Other Becketts*, Beckett has become a popular culture icon in the 21st century. Voigts-Virchow argued that Beckett's influence can be seen in unlikely places—for instance, he appeared on large billboards and in magazine ads for

Apple's Think Different campaign, as well as in the children's show *Teletubbies*.

In the last few years, we have seen Beckett go viral. Facebook has pages and groups dedicated to Beckett, such as The Samuel Beckett Endpage, Samuel Beckett and World Literature, and The Letters of Samuel Beckett. The embarrassing video of Beckett on vacation which was turned into a mock 70s Cop Show went viral and the image of a thin Beckett wearing shorts became the poster of Beckett sessions and conferences, particularly those in tropical climates. Most amusing are the comics and memes that pop up every so often; they are nearly always of *Waiting for Godot*—two tramps, a stone, and a tree. The image that originates from W. B. Yeats's *Purgatory* is always attributed to Beckett's *Waiting for Godot*. And, the play's opening image is used to comment on politics and modern mobile devices, but ironically, it is rarely used to critique religion or prison systems.

Samuel Beckett, who attempted to live a private life despite his fame, ironically also left us with a legacy through his letters, his manuscript drafts, and professional photographs of him. These archived traces and the power of his minimal, radical works on stage and in print will ensure that his legacy continues like embers that glow in the dark.

Endnotes

Introduction: "Astride of a grave and a difficult birth": Samuel Beckett's beginning

1. Beckett revealed that he was born on Friday, the 13th and Good Friday in a 1962 letter he wrote to his American publisher. In response to Barney Rosset's birthday card, Beckett wrote: "Very touched by your card and remembrance. I was born on Good Friday 13th, so can't share your high opinion of the conjunction. And yet when I have the courage to take a quick look back I can see that the miracles haven't been wanting and that but for them it's in the better place I'd be for this long time." See Dirk Van Hulle and Pim Verhulst's blog for Bloomsbury's celebration of Beckett's birthday (April 13, 2019). However, Eoin O'Brien questions whether this is really so. He posits that while April 13, 1906 is the date internationally accepted as his birthdate because that is when Beckett says he was born, it is likely that he was born on May 13, 1906. Beckett's father had his birthdate registered as May 13, 1906. The paperwork was filed on June 14, 1906. It was common that the birth certificate was created about a month after the birth, not two months later (The Beckett Country, p. 1). Knowlson cautions about making too much of this discrepancy, asserting that the Becketts celebrated Samuel's birthday on April 13th and that, after all, is what matters (Damned to Fame, pp. 23-4).

2. Beckett grew up in the Dublin suburb, in a house that teemed with respectable bourgeois security. His parents had hoped that Beckett would take over the quantity surveying business, located on Clare Street in Dublin. However, Beckett found that the "financial security" the business would afford him would dry up his creative individuality. Indeed, he witnessed his brother, Frank, who

returned from India to run the family business, falling into conformity (Bates, *Beckett's Art of Salvage*, p. 33).

3. Beckett traveled to Germany during the thirties, visiting galleries and keeping his ears attuned to the Nazi propaganda. His diaries of the time, as Mark Nixon in "Between Gospel and Prohibition: Beckett in Nazi Germany 1936-1937" reveals, are deeply concerned with the politics and atrocities that Germany was steamrolling towards (31-47).

4. Martha Dow Fehsenfeld and Lois More Overbeck, eds. *The Letters of Samuel Beckett: 1929-1940* (Cambridge UP, 2009), p. 520.

Chapter 1 – *Le Kid, Human Wishes, Eleuthéria*: "we might well ring down the curtain."

1. Samuel Beckett, "Sean O'Casey," in Disjecta: Miscellaneous Writings and a Dramatic Fragment, ed. Ruby Cohn (Grove P, 1984), p. 82.

2. Lady Gregory, founding member of the Abbey Theatre, quoted in John P. Harrington, ed., *Modern and Contemporary Irish Drama* (Norton, 2009), p. 402.

3. In Bates's discussion of comic bowlers in Beckett's writing, she traces Beckett's interest to music halls and comic silent films back to his childhood: "Beckett's uncle Howard brought him to the cinema in Dun Laoghaire and Dublin, passing on an enduring enthusiasm for Charlie Chaplin, Laurel and Hardy, Buster Keaton and Harold Lloyd" (*Beckett's Art of Salvage*, p. 41).

4. Knowlson, *Damned to Fame*, p. 250.

5. In his conversation with art critic Georges Duthuit, Beckett famously asserted that the artist has "nothing to express, nothing

with which to express, nothing from which to express, no power to express, no desire to express, together with the obligation to express." See Samuel Beckett, "Three Dialogues," in *Disjecta: Miscellaneous Writings and a Dramatic Fragment*, ed. Ruby Cohn (Grove P, 1984), p. 139.

Chapter 2 – *Waiting for Godot* and *Endgame*: Place and History on the Absurdist Stage

1. Bruce Weber, "Ruby Cohn, Writer and Expert on Beckett, Dies at 89." *The New York Times*. October 30, 2011.

2. Bianchini is the first to fully examine Alan Schneider's contribution to bringing Beckett to American audiences. Drawing on Schneider and Beckett archival materials which include conversations and correspondences between Schneider and Beckett, she reconstructs, not only Schneider's productions of Beckett but also the process and reception of the works.

3. Upon learning of Hitler's death, de Valera wrote a eulogy for Germany's fallen tyrant.

4. See interview with Paul Chan in Rob Reginio, David Houston Jones, and Katherine Weiss, eds., *Samuel Beckett and Contemporary Art* (Ibidem P, 2017), pp. 293-314.

5. Pozzo's memory of watching Lucky dance recalls the dehumanization of extreme power. Similar scenes have been reconstructed in movies such as the 2015 Holocaust movie *Son of Saul* and the 2013 movie *Twelve Years a Slave*.

6. Marjorie Perloff in her essay charts Beckett's flight from the Gestapo and Julie Bates reveals in her study of boots that in the original French version of *Waiting for Godot*, Gogo and Didi

reminisce about wondering in the Pyrenees. The reference points to the dangers that Beckett and Déchevaux-Dumesnil faced. The Pyrenees, a notorious escape route during the War, leading from France and to Spain, was rough and dangerous terrain. Beckett's references to real places are those that nearly always have the residue of the Second World War.

Chapter 3 – *Krapp's Last Tape*, *That Time*, *Ohio Impromptu*: Remembering That Time, That Place

1. In *Eleuthéria* the protagonist Victor Krap, too, is a struggling writer. While his father gave up writing for a bourgeois life, Victor is in a state of depression, lethargic, and unable to write. Rather than aligning his creative malady with constipation as Beckett does in *Krapp's Last Tape*, Beckett's earlier Krap suffers from an inability to urinate.

2. Seán Kennedy, "Does Beckett Studies Require a Subject? Mourning Ireland in the *Texts for Nothing*," in *Samuel Beckett: History, Memory, Archive*, ed. Seán Kennedy and Katherine Weiss (Palgrave/Macmillan, 2009), p. 12. Anthony Cronin, James Knowlson, and Julie Bates have also written extensively on images of fathers walking with their sons. See Anthony Cronin, *Samuel Beckett: The Last Modernist* (Harper Collins, 1997), pp. 28-31; Knowlson, *Damned to Fame*, p. 33; and Bates, *Beckett's Art of Salvage*, pp. 75-9.

3. Bates steers away from the word "exile" since Beckett often returned to Ireland while his parents and brother still lived (pp. 61-3).

4. In *Molloy* the protagonist describes the non-verbal form of communication he uses when visiting his mother: "I got into communication with her by knocks on her skull. One knock meant

yes, two no, three I don't know, four money, five goodbye. ... I looked for and finally found a more efficient means of putting the idea of money into her head. This consisted of replacing the four knocks of my index-knuckle by one or more (according to my needs) thumps of the fist, on her skull" (p. 18). In 1947 Beckett depicts the attempts to communicate with his feeble mother through the frenzied, albeit comedic voice of the vagrant Molloy. Nearly four decades later, this form of non-verbal communication returns, now without humor.

Chapter 4 – *All That Fall, Happy Days, Footfalls, Not I*: "Spared Love": The Trauma of Being Seen; the Trauma of Being Unseen

1. For Julie Bates, the movement of the rocking chair in Beckett identifies "restful sleep with desired death." The rocking chair generates, she continues, "much of the ambivalence around death" in Beckett's work from *Murphy* to *Rockaby*. See Bates, *Beckett's Art of Salvage*, p. 107.

Chapter 5 – Acts without words: Avoiding the danger zone in Beckett's *Act Without Words I, Act Without Words II, Film, Quad*, and *What Where*

1. Beckett stage direction recurs numerous times of the mime. As such, no page numbers will be provided here.

2. In *Frescoes of the Skull: The Later Prose and Drama of Samuel Beckett*, James Knowlson provided an essential look into Beckett's interest in Heinrich von Kleist's study of the marionette on stage. Knowlson showed how the movement of the actors in Beckett's

television plays echo the movements of marionettes on 19th-century stages (277-85). This same marionette movement is evident in Beckett's mimes.

3. Bates recalled that "Beckett's uncle Howard brought him to the cinema in Dun Laoghaire and Dublin, passing on an enduring enthusiasm for Charlie Chaplin, Laurel and Hardy, Buster Keaton and Harold Lloyd" (41-2).

4. In *Frescoes of the Skull*, Knowlson stated that "Their hands form, in fact, the pattern of an unbroken chain, an emblem that, traditionally, has been used to symbolize eternity" (122).

5. Beckett was particularly fond of Dante's *Purgatorio*, a text he studied as a student. See Daniela Caselli, *Beckett's Dantes: Intertexuality in the Fiction and Criticism* (Manchester UP, 2005).

6. The Beckett on Film version of *Play*, directed by Anthony Minghella, reimagined Beckett's 1962 work in purgatory, with other bodies trapped in urns, recalling their past regressions to someday be released. While his interpretation is a clever reading of *Play*, the stage version is much less explicitly a retelling of Dante's damned than *Quad* appears to be. These works differ, too, in that *Play* clearly provides us with the back-story of each character and how they are interrelated. *Quad* has no such dialogue or monologue.

7. See Herren's *Samuel Beckett's Plays* for a discussion that brings some of these allusions to light.

Chapter 6 – Beckett's Legacy

1. Sam Shepard often spoke of Beckett's influence over his dramatic works. See, for example, *Sam Shepard: Stalking Himself*, dir. Oren Jacoby (Great Performances, 1998) and *This So-Called Disaster*, dir. Michael Almereyda (MGM, 2003).

Sources

Abbott, H. Porter. *Beckett Writing Beckett: The Author in the Autograph.* Cornell UP, 1996.

Anderton, Joseph. *Beckett's Creature: Art of Failure after the Holocaust.* Bloomsbury, 2016.

Astier, Pierre. "Beckett's Ohio Impromptu: A View from the Isle of Swans." *Modern Drama,* Vol. 25, No. 3, 1982, pp. 331-41.

Bair, Deidre. *Samuel Beckett: A Biography.* Harcourt, 1978.

Bates, Julie. *Beckett's Art of Salvage: Writing and Material Imagination, 1932-1987.* Cambridge UP, 2017.

Beckett, Samuel. *Acts Without Words I. The Complete Dramatic Works.* Faber and Faber, 1990, pp. 201-06.

Beckett, Samuel. *Acts Without Words II. The Complete Dramatic Works.* Faber and Faber, 1990, pp. 207-11.

Beckett, Samuel. *All That Fall. The Complete Dramatic Works.* Faber and Faber, 1990, pp. 169-99.

Beckett, Samuel. *... but the clouds .... The Complete Dramatic Works.* Faber and Faber, 1990, pp. 415-22.

Beckett, Samuel. "The Capital of the Ruins." *The Complete Short Prose 1929-1989.* Grove P, 1995, pp. 275-8.

Beckett, Samuel. *Come and Go. The Complete Dramatic Works.* Faber and Faber, 1990, pp. 351-57.

Beckett, Samuel. "Dante ... Bruno . Vico .. Joyce." *Disjecta: Miscellaneous Writings and a Dramatic Fragment.* Ed. Ruby Cohn. Grove P, 1984, pp. 19-33.

Beckett, Samuel. *Eh Joe. The Complete Dramatic Works.* Faber and Faber, 1990, pp. 359-67.

Beckett, Samuel. *Eleuthéria.* Fox Rock, Inc. 1995.

Beckett, Samuel. *Endgame. The Complete Dramatic Works.* Faber and Faber, 1990, pp. 89-134.

Beckett, Samuel. *Film. The Complete Dramatic Works.* Faber and Faber, 1990, pp. 321-34.

Beckett, Samuel. "First Love." *The Complete Short Prose 1929-1989.* Grove P, 1995, pp. 25-45.

Beckett, Samuel. *Footfalls. The Complete Dramatic Works.* Faber and Faber, 1990, pp. 397-403.

Beckett, Samuel. *Ghost Trio. The Complete Dramatic Works.* Faber and Faber, 1990, pp. 405-14.

Beckett, Samuel. *Happy Days. The Complete Dramatic Works.* Faber and Faber, 1990, pp. 135-68.

Beckett, Samuel. *Human Wishes. Disjecta: Miscellaneous Writings and a Dramatic Fragment.* Ed. Ruby Cohn. Grove P, 1984, pp. 153-66.

Beckett, Samuel. *Krapp's Last Tape. The Complete Dramatic Works.* Faber and Faber, 1990, pp. 213-23.

Beckett, Samuel. *Nohow On: Company, Ill Seen Ill Said, Worstward Ho.* Grove P, 1996.

Beckett, Samuel. *Not I. The Complete Dramatic Works.* Faber and Faber, 1990, pp. 369-83.

Beckett, Samuel. *Ohio Impromptu. The Complete Dramatic Works.* Faber and Faber, 1990, pp. 443-48.

Beckett, Samuel. *A Piece of Monologue. The Complete Dramatic Works.* Faber and Faber, 1990, pp. 423-30.

Beckett, Samuel. *Quad. The Complete Dramatic Works.* Faber and Faber, 1990, pp. 449-54.

Beckett, Samuel. *Rockaby. The Complete Dramatic Works.* Faber and Faber, 1990, pp. 431-42.

Beckett, Samuel. "Sean O'Casey." *Disjecta: Miscellaneous Writings and a Dramatic Fragment.* Ed. Ruby Cohn. Grove P, 1984, pp. 82-84.

Beckett, Samuel. *That Time. The Complete Dramatic Works.* Faber and Faber, 1990, pp. 385-95.

Beckett, Samuel. "Three Dialogues." *Disjecta: Miscellaneous Writings and a Dramatic Fragment.* Ed. Ruby Cohn. Grove P, 1984, pp. 138-45.

Beckett, Samuel. *Three Novels: Molloy, Malone Dies, The Unnamable.* Grove, 1958.

Beckett, Samuel. *Waiting for Godot. The Complete Dramatic Works.* Faber and Faber, 1990, pp. 7-88.

Beckett, Samuel. *What Where*. *The Complete Dramatic Works*. Faber and Faber, 1990, pp. 467-76.

Bennett, Michael. *Reassessing the Theatre of the Absurd: Camus, Beckett, Ionesco, Genet, and Pinter*. Palgrave/ Macmillan, 2011.

Ben-Zvi, Linda. *Women in Beckett: Performance and Critical Perspectives*. U of Illinois P, 1990.

Ben-Zvi, Linda. "Not I: Through a Tube Starkly." *Samuel Beckett*. Ed. Jennifer Birkett and Kate Ince. Longman, 2000, pp. 259-65.

Bianchini, Natka. *Samuel Beckett's Theatre in America: The Legacy of Alan Schneider as Beckett's American Director*. Palgrave/ Macmillan, 2015.

Blackman, Jackie. "Beckett's Theatre: 'After Auschwitz.'" *Samuel Beckett: Memory, History, Archive*. Eds. Seán Kennedy and Katherine Weiss. Palgrave/Macmillan, 2009, pp. 71-88.

Campbell, Julie. "The Semantic Krapp in *Krapp's Last Tape*." *Samuel Beckett Today/Aujourd'hui: An Annual Bilingual Review/Revue Annuelle Bilingue*, Vol. 6, 1997, pp. 63-72.

Carville, Conor. *Samuel Beckett and the Visual Arts*. Cambridge UP, 2018.

Caselli, Daniela. *Beckett's Dantes: Intertexuality in the Fiction and Criticism*. Manchester U P, 2005.

Cohn, Ruby. *A Beckett Canon: An Indispensable Guide to the Oeuvre of Samuel Beckett, Spanning Sixty Years*. U of Michigan P, 2005.

Cohn, Ruby. *Back to Beckett*. Princeton UP, 1973.

Cohn, Ruby. *Just Play: Beckett's Theater*. Princeton UP, 1980.

Cohn, Ruby. *Samuel Beckett: The Comic Gamut*. Rutgers UP, 1962.

Connor, Steven. "Looping the Loop: Tape Time in Burroughs and Beckett." Talk given at the University of Iowa. January 28, 2010. www.stevenconnor.com.

Connor, Steven. *Paraphernalia: The Curious Lives of Magical Things*. Profile, 2012.

Cronin, Anthony. *Samuel Beckett: The Last Modernist*. Harper Collins, 1997.

Esslin, Martin. *The Theatre of the Absurd*, 3rd edition. Penguin, 1980.

Fehsenfeld, Martha Dow and Lois More Overbeck, eds. *The Letters of Samuel Beckett: 1929-1940*. Cambridge UP, 2009.

Fehsenfeld, Martha Dow, George Craig, Dan Gunn, and Lois More Overbeck, eds. *The Letters of Samuel Beckett: 1957-1965*. Cambridge UP, 2014.

Fletcher, John, et. al. *A Student's Guide to the Plays of Samuel Beckett*. Faber, 1978.

Gaffney, Phyllis. *Healing Amid the Ruins: The Irish Hospital at Saint-Lô (1945-46)*. A&A Farmar, 1999.

Germoni, Karine. "From Joyce to Beckett: The Beckettian Dramatic Interior Monologue." *Journal of Beckett Studies*, Vol. 13, No. 2, 2005, pp. 137-49.

Gilman, Richard. "Beckett." *Parisian Review*, Vol. 41, 1974, pp. 56-76.

Gontarski, S. E. *The Edinburgh Companion to Samuel Beckett and the Arts*. Edinburgh UP, 2014.

Gontarski, S. E. *The Intent of Undoing in Samuel Beckett's Dramatic Texts*. Indiana UP, 1985.

Gregory, Lady. "Our Irish Theatre." *Modern and Contemporary Irish Drama*. Ed. John P. Harrington. Norton, 2009, pp. 401-09.

Gussow, Mel. "Stage: Disputed 'Endgame' in Debut." *The New York Times*. December 20, 1984.

Harmon, Maurice. *No Author Better Serve: The Correspondence of Samuel Beckett and Alan Schneider*. Harvard UP, 1998.

Haynes, John and James Knowlson. *Images of Beckett*. Cambridge UP, 2003.

Herren, Graley. *Samuel Beckett's Plays on Film and Television*. Palgrave/Macmillan, 2007.

Jones, David Houston. *Samuel Beckett and Testimony*. Palgrave/Macmillan, 2011.

Joyce, James. *Dubliners*. Grafton Books, 1987.

Joyce, James. *Ulysses*. Random House, 1992.

Kalb, Jonathan. *Beckett in Performance*. Cambridge UP, 1989.

Kennedy, Seán and Katherine Weiss, eds. *Samuel Beckett: History, Memory, Archive*. Palgrave/Macmillan, 2009.

Kennedy, Seán. "Does Beckett Studies Require a Subject? Mourning Ireland in the *Texts for Nothing*." Ed. Seán Kennedy and Katherine Weiss. *Samuel Beckett: History, Memory, Archive*. Palgrave/Macmillan, 2009, pp. 11-30.

Kleinberg-Levin, David. *Beckett's Words: The Promise of Happiness in a Time of Mourning*. Bloomsbury, 2015.

Knowlson, James. *Damned to Fame: The Life of Samuel Beckett*. Simon and Schuster, 1996.

Knowlson, James and John Pilling. *Frescoes of the Skull: The Later Prose and Drama of Samuel Beckett*. Grove P, 1980.

Knowlson, James and Elizabeth Knowlson, eds. *Beckett Remembering, Remembering Beckett: A Centenary Celebration*. Arcade, 2006.

LaCapra, Dominick. *Writing History, Writing Trauma*. Johns Hopkins UP, 2001.

Lawley, Paul. "The Excluded Child: Brian Friel's *Faith Healer* and Beckett's *Endgame*." *Samuel Beckett Today/Aujourd'hui*, Vol. 21, 2009, pp. 151-63.

Lawley, Paul. "Stages of Identity: From *Krapp's Last Tape* to *Play*." *The Cambridge Companion to Beckett*. Ed. John Pilling. Cambridge UP, 1994, pp. 88-105.

Lloyd, David. *Beckett's Thing: Painting and Theatre*. Edinburgh UP, 2016.

Lyons, W. H. "Backtracking Beckett." *Literature and Society: Studies in Nineteenth and Twentieth Century French Literature, Presented to R.J. North*. Ed. C.A. Burns. John Goodman & Sons, 1980, pp. 214-20.

McDonagh, Martin. *The Beauty Queen of Leenane and Other Plays*. Vintage Books, 1998.

McMullan, Audrey. "Samuel Beckett's *Cette Fois*: Between Time(s) and Space(s)." *French Studies*, Vol. 44, No. 4, 1990, pp. 424-39.

Mehta, Xerxes. "'Down, all going down ...': The Spiral Structure of Beckett's Theater." *A Companion to Samuel Beckett*. Ed. S.E. Gontarski. Wiley-Blackwell, 2010, pp. 372-88.

Mercier, Vivian. "The Uneventful Event (1956)." *Critical Essays on*

Samuel Beckett: Critical Thought Series 4. Ed. Lance St. John Butler. Scolar P, 1993, pp. 29-30.

Nixon, Mark. "Between Gospel and Prohibition: Beckett in Nazi Germany 1936-1937." *Samuel Beckett: History, Memory, Archive*. Ed. Seán Kennedy and Katherine Weiss. Palgrave/Macmillan, 2009, pp. 31-47.

Nixon, Mark. *Samuel Beckett's German Diaries, 1936-1937*. Continuum, 2011.

Nixon, Mark and Dirk van Hulle. *Samuel Beckett's Library*. Cambridge UP, 2017.

Pattie, David. *The Complete Critical Guide to Samuel Beckett*. Routledge, 2000.

Perloff, Marjorie. "'In Love with Hiding': Samuel Beckett's War." *Iowa Review*, Vol. 35 No. 2, 2005, pp. 76-103.

Pountney, Rosemary. *Theatre of Shadows: Samuel Beckett's Drama 1956-1976*. Colin Smythe, 1988.

O'Brien, Eoin. *The Beckett Country*. The Black Cat P, 1986.

Reginio, Rob. "Samuel Beckett, the Archive, and the Problem of History." *Samuel Beckett: Memory, History, Archive*. Ed. Seán Kennedy and Katherine Weiss. Palgrave/Macmillan, 2009, pp. 111-128.

Reginio, Rob, David Houston Jones, and Katherine Weiss, eds. *Samuel Beckett and Contemporary Art*. Ibidem P, 2017.

Rodriguez-Gago, Antonia. "The Embodiment of Memory (and Forgetting) in Beckett's Late Women's Play." *Assaph: Studies in the Theatre*, No. 17-18, 2003, pp. 113-26.

Scarry, Elaine. *The Body in Pain: The Making and Unmaking of the World*. Oxford UP, 1985.

Seelig, Adam. "Beckett's Dying Remains: The Process of Playwriting in the *Ohio Impromptu* Manuscripts." *Modern Drama*, Vol. 43 No. 3, 2000, pp. 376-92.

Shakespeare, William. *Hamlet*. Folger, 2012.

Shenker, Israel. "Interview with Samuel Beckett." *The New York Times*. May 6, 1956.

Tanaka, Mariko Hori, Yoshiki Tajiri, Michiko Tsushima, and Robert Eaglestone. *Beckett and Trauma*. Manchester UP, 2018.

Thomson, Stephen. "'It's not my fault sir': The Child, Presence and Stage Space in Beckett's Theatre." *Samuel Beckett Today/Aujourd'hui*, Vol. 15, 2005, pp. 261-70.

Tranter, Rhys. "'Without Solution of Continuity': Beckett's *That Time* and Trauma Memoir." *Samuel Beckett Today/Aujourd'hui*, Vol. 27, 2015, pp. 115-28.

van Hulle, Dirk. *The New Cambridge Companion to Samuel Beckett*. Cambridge UP, 2015.

Voigts-Virchow, Eckhart. "Face Values: Beckett, Inc. The Camera Plays, and Cultural Liminality." *Other Becketts*. Ed. Daniela Caselli, Steven Connor, and Laura Salisbury. Journal of Beckett Studies Books, 2002, pp. 119-35.

Voigts-Virchow, Eckhart. "*Quad I* and Teletubbies or: 'Aisthetic' Panopticism versus Reading Beckett." *Samuel Beckett Today/Aujourd'hui*, Vol. 11, 2001, pp. 210-18.

Weber, Bruce. "Ruby Cohn, Writer and Expert on Beckett, Dies at 89." *The New York Times*. October 30, 2011.

Weiss, Katherine. *The Plays of Samuel Beckett*. Methuen Drama, 2012.

Weiss, Katherine. "Bits and Pieces: The Fragmented Body in Samuel Beckett's *Not I* and *That Time*." *Other Becketts*. Ed. Daniela Caselli, Steven Connor, and Laura Salisbury. Journal of Beckett Studies Books, 2002, pp. 187-95.

Whitelaw, Billie. *Billie Whitelaw ...: Who He?* St. Martin's P, 1996.

Williams, Tennessee. *A Streetcar Named Desire*. New Directions, 2014.

Withers, Jeremy and Daniel Shea. *Culture on Two Wheels: The Bicycle in Literature and Film*. U of Nebraska P, 2016.

Woolfe, Zachary. "Critic's Pick, Review: A 92-Year-Old's 'Endgame' Opera Is Patiently Perfect." *The New York Times*, November 16, 2018.

Yeats, William Butler and Lady Augusta Gregory. *Cathleen ni Houlihan. Modern and Contemporary Irish Drama*. Ed. John P. Harrington. Norton, 2009, pp. 3-11.

Yeats, William Butler. "The Lake Isle of Innisfree." *The Norton Anthology of English Literature.* Ed. Stephen Greenblatt. Volume F, 9th Edition. Norton, 2012, p. 2087.

Yeats, William Butler. *Purgatory. Modern and Contemporary Irish Drama.* Ed. John P. Harrington. Norton, 2009, pp. 29-35.

Yeats, William Butler. "Sailing to Byzantium." *The Norton Anthology of English Literature.* Ed. Stephen Greenblatt. Volume F, 9th Edition. Norton, 2012, p. 2102.

Suggested Reading

The earliest writings on Samuel Beckett appeared in the 1950s. These consist mainly of theater reviews in magazines, newspapers, and literary journals. Although the articles were often not favorable to Beckett, the fact that these reviews appeared in places like *The Times Literary Supplement*, *The New York Times*, and in literary journals like *Modern Drama*, which is still producing some of the top scholarship on 20th and 21st-century drama and theater, speaks to the importance of Beckett's often-criticized work.

Of particular note, the journal *Perspectives* had dedicated an entire volume to Beckett in 1959. This volume includes articles by Beckett's first academic advocates, namely Ruby Cohn, Edith Kern, Hugh Kenner, and Jean-Jacques Mayoux, among others. Many of these scholars would become leading academics in the field of Beckett studies. They saw the importance of the writer who still incited doubts in some critics. Beckett's literary career had a slow start (his early prose was rejected by publishers and *Waiting for Godot* was not favorably received); however, he had become one of our most important playwrights. By providing compelling plays that do not follow dramatic conventions, Beckett freed playwrights in similar ways to how James Joyce's experimental prose freed fiction writers.

Most notably, Ruby Cohn had written some of the best Beckett scholarship in her career that ranged from 1959 to 2005. *Samuel Beckett: The Comic Gamut* (Rutgers UP, 1962), *Back to Beckett* (Princeton UP, 1973), and *Just Play: Beckett's Theater* (Princeton UP, 1980) provide an insightful humanist approach to the author. Her final book, *A Beckett Canon*, is essential reading for the Beckett scholar. It provides a catalog of Beckett's complete work and traces the origins and allusions in those works.

Another early scholar in Beckett studies, Martin Esslin, wrote one of the most influential books on Beckett. His *The Theatre of* the *Absurd* (1961), often cited and forever linking Beckett to the idea of the Absurd, is an attempt to understand post-World War II European plays. Esslin's concept of absurdist theater as it pertains to Beckett is much debated by Beckett scholars such as Michael Bennett in his 2011 book *Reassessing the Theatre of the Absurd: Camus, Beckett, Ionesco, Genet, and Pinter* (Palgrave/Macmillan). It is unclear to many how authors as different as Samuel Beckett, Arthur Adamov, Eugène Ionesco, Jean Genet, and Harold Pinter comfortably stand under the umbrella of the Absurd. What is more, Beckett's plays do not remain static in regards to aesthetic and formal structures.

S. E. Gontarski, an American academic, discovered a unique trend in Beckett's manuscripts. Instead of adding to his work as he wrote, Beckett seemed to be erasing details. This process is explored in Gontarski's *The Intent of Undoing in Samuel Beckett's Dramatic Texts* (Indiana UP, 1985). This book led the way to fully conceiving Beckett, not as an Absurdist, but rather a minimalist. Other manuscript studies that Gontarski, along with Dougald McMillan, and James Knowlson edited are *The Theatrical Notebooks of Samuel Beckett*, a series of books published by Faber which reproduce and examine the written notes Beckett made and used when he was directing his plays. Dirk van Hulle and Mark Nixon are in the process of making Beckett's manuscripts increasingly accessible to scholars. It is the hope that with their impressive Digital Manuscript Project, one day scholars who are unable to travel to Austin, Texas or Reading, UK can still access archival material in a manner that is no longer beholden of place.

Scholarship in Beckett studies was slow to incorporate biographical explorations. This is no doubt the result of Beckett's reserved nature and intense wish for privacy. And, even though there were many, like Ruby Cohn, who had formed a friendship with the author, the first to attempt to undertake the challenge of recording his life was Deirdre Bair. Her unauthorized biography, neither helped nor hindered by Beckett, was published in 1978. *Samuel Beckett: A Biography* (Harcourt) is a necessary failure. James

Knowlson, the only authorized biographer, began publishing on Beckett in 1971. His early work, particularly *Frescoes of the Skull: The Later Prose and Drama of Samuel Beckett*, which he co-authored with John Pilling (Grove, 1980), provides insightful interpretations of Beckett's plays. Knowlson drew on the published and staged texts as well as the manuscript drafts which he had helped to secure in what is now the Samuel Beckett International Foundation.

Knowlson's biography of Beckett, *Damned to Fame: The Life of Samuel Beckett* (Simon & Schuster, 1996), has forever changed Beckett studies. *Damned to Fame* completes the portrait that Bair and others attempted to create. But unlike Bair and others, Beckett helped Knowlson, providing him with access to unpublished literary works and letters. Knowlson reconstructed Beckett's life, also revealing Beckett's deep concern over the rise of fascism, his work with the Resistance, his extreme generosity towards friends and causes he believed in, and his struggles with his mental and physical health. A year after Knowlson's book appeared, Anthony Cronin's biography *Samuel Beckett: The Last Modernist* (Harper Collins, 1997) was published. As the *New York Times* reviewer, Morris Dickstein noted, Knowlson's biography is a "definitive piece of scholarship," whereas Cronin's biography holds "novelistic flair."

While Bair and Cronin are read and cited by Beckett scholars, Knowlson's biography opened the door to numerous projects, including Maurice Harmon's *No Author Better Served: The Correspondence of Samuel Beckett and Alan Schneider* (Harvard UP, 1998), Phyllis Gaffney's *Healing Amid the Ruins: The Irish Hospital at Saint-Lô (1945-46)* (A&A Farmar, 1999), Mark Nixon's *Samuel Beckett's German Diaries, 1936-1937* (Continuum, 2011), Natka Bianchini's *Samuel Beckett's Theatre in America: The Legacy of Alan Schneider as Beckett's American Director* (Palgrave/Macmillan, 2015), Mark Nixon and Dirk van Hulle's *Samuel Beckett's Library* (Cambridge UP, 2017), and *The Letters of Samuel Beckett* (a four-volume collection published by Cambridge UP). Knowlson's other notable books are *Beckett Remembering/Remembering Beckett: A Centenary*

Celebration (ed. with Elizabeth Knowlson, Arcade, 2006) and with John Haynes *Images of Beckett* (Cambridge UP, 2003).

Notable are works that explore Beckett, trauma, and the Holocaust. Knowlson's biography has continued to lead scholars to explore Beckett's work in the aftermath of World War II. Seán Kennedy and Katherine Weiss, ed. *Samuel Beckett: History, Memory, Archive* (Palgrave/Macmillan, 2009) contains several essays that explore Beckett and historical trauma. Noteworthy, too, are David Houston Jones's *Samuel Beckett and Testimony* (Palgrave/ Macmillan, 2011), David Kleinberg-Levin's *Beckett's Words: The Promise of Happiness in a Time of Mourning* (Bloomsbury, 2015), Joseph Anderton's *Beckett's Creature: Art of Failure after the Holocaust* (Bloomsbury, 2016), Mariko Hori Tanaka, Yoshiki Tajiri, Michiko Tsushima, and Robert Eaglestone's *Beckett and Trauma* (Manchester UP, 2018).

In these last few years, there has been an influx of works that deal with Beckett and art,–notably Conor Carville's *Samuel Beckett and the Visual Arts* (Cambridge UP, 2018), David Lloyd's *Beckett's Thing: Painting and Theatre* (Edinburgh UP, 2016), and S.E. Gontarski's *The Edinburgh Companion to Samuel Beckett and the Arts* (Edinburgh UP, 2014). These works are all in some way inspired by Knowlson and Haynes's *Images of Beckett*, as well as archival research that has given us insight into what artworks Beckett saw. In *Samuel Beckett and Contemporary Art* (Ibidem, 2017), Reginio, Jones, and Weiss collected essays that explore the imprint that Beckett has left on 21st-century artists.

Literary scholarship sometimes verges too heavily on the philosophical. In recent years, there have been a few studies that have refreshingly turned to concrete objects that have been shown on stage or described in Beckett's prose. This line of research stems from discussions around Beckett's use of the tape recorder, but scholars like Julie Bates have taken this materialist approach further in her book, *Beckett's Art of Salvage: Writing and Material Imagination, 1932-1987* (Cambridge UP, 2017). Others of note are Jeremy Withers and Daniel Shea's *Culture on Two Wheels: The*

Bicycle in Literature and Film (U of Nebraska P, 2016) and Steven Connor's *Paraphernalia: The Curious Lives of Magical Things* (Profile, 2012).

There are numerous volumes and monographs published on all aspects of Beckett's life and work. In fact, the Modern Language Association's bibliography database lists nearly 7,000 works on Beckett since 1950. In the last five years, there have been roughly 850 published works on Beckett and 23 unpublished dissertations. There is still much to write about the minimalist author, Samuel Beckett.

About the Author

Katherine Weiss is Professor of English at East Tennessee State University. Her books, as author or editor, include *Samuel Beckett and Contemporary Art* (2017), *The Plays of Samuel Beckett* (2013), and *Samuel Beckett: History, Memory, Archive* (2009). Weiss has frequently given academic talks on drama and Samuel Beckett, and has directed *Waiting for Godot*, *Come and Go*, and *Footfalls* at ETSU. Weiss is a board member of the Samuel Beckett Society.

A Word from the Publisher

Thank you for reading *Simply Beckett*!

If you enjoyed reading it, we would be grateful if you could help others discover and enjoy it too.

Please review it with your favorite book provider such as Amazon, BN, Kobo, iBooks and Goodreads, among others.

Again, thank you for your support and we look forward to offering you more great reads.

Made in the USA
Monee, IL
12 November 2020

47368045R00080